DOG TRAINING
MADE EASY

DOG TRAINING
MADE EASY

Michael Tucker

HOWELL BOOK HOUSE INC.
230 Park Avenue, New York, N.Y. 10169

National Library of Australia
Cataloguing-in-Publication entry

Tucker, Michael.
  Dog training made easy.
  Index
  ISBN 0 7270 1227 4
  1. Dogs—Training—Handbook, manuals, etc.
  I. Title.

636.7'08'3

Distributed in America and Canada
by Howell Book House Inc.
230 Park Avenue, New York, N.Y. 10169

RIGBY PUBLISHERS • ADELAIDE
SYDNEY • MELBOURNE • BRISBANE
NEW YORK • LONDON • AUCKLAND
First published 1980
Reprinted in paper back 1983
Reprinted in 1984
Copyright © 1980 Michael Tucker
All rights reserved

Typeset by ProComp Productions Pty Ltd, Adelaide
Printed in Singapore by Kyodo-Shing Loong Printing Industries Pte Ltd

Contents

Acknowledgments

I wish to thank Professor D. C. Blood, B.V.Sc., F.A.C.V.Sc., Professor of Veterinary Medicine, University of Melbourne, for his very kind remarks in the Foreword he has written for this book. My grateful thanks go to Mr Keith Batchelor, A.R.M.I.T., who produced all the photographs for this book—his patience and expertise were second to none in the hours he spent in producing these excellent visual aids. I also thank all those owners who supplied the numerous breeds for him to photograph. I am indebted to the Reverend Father Matthew G. F. Peiris, Ph.D., for all the information he gave me regarding dogs sensing evil spirits, and to Mrs Irene Knight for her experience on the same subject. My sincere thanks go to Professor A. Stock, M.D., Ph.D., Medical Professor at the Free University, Amsterdam for his valuable contribution in respect of dogs' scenting powers, and to Mr David Churchman, formerly Chief Inspector and Chief Instructor at the London Metropolitan Police Dog Training Establishment, who has also contributed to the same subject. I also thank Dr Ian W. Bradney, B.V.Sc., M.A.C.V.Sc., for his advice on veterinary matters and Professor T. J. Pickvance, M.A., B.Sc., for his work in studying canine behaviour. I shall always be grateful to the countless number of people with whom I have associated over the many years in the obedience dog world, the Royal Air Force Police, the Guide Dog movement and those engaged in training dogs in the Police Forces. Finally, I wish to thank Eunice Smith, Vonda Wiebenga, Glenda Farmer, and my wife Valerie for doing the typing.

Foreword

The love that a human being can have for a dog and, one suspects, the love that a dog can have for a human, is one of the most wonderful experiences in life. And the complete enjoyment of that relationship depends on mutual trust, a relationship of quality between unequal beings. Michael Tucker is one of those lucky people who can see things from a dog's point of view. As a result he can describe the many obstacles that can occur in the way of establishing the bond of confidence between dog and man, the bond of confidence on which mutual trust can be built.

Not only must the dog trust the human, but the human must know the limitations of trust and affection that a dog can experience. This is because there are limits, limits on both sides, and avoidance of inevitable clashes is essential if the confidence bond is to survive. It is the constant reinforcement of that bond which marks the complete dog trainer. And Michael Tucker demonstrates that faculty admirably in this book. Every aspect of a dog's life, every possible situation that can arise between human and canine friends, is examined carefully, the pitfalls described, and the method of avoiding them set out.

The subject matter of this book is dealt with simply and concisely, and without the psychological overtones with which it might have been vested. It sets out solely to guide the dog owner to the stage of mutual confidence where a real bond of affection can then arise. To an extent this depends on the author's experience as a trainer of guide dogs for the blind, because there is nowhere in human–animal relations in which the establishment of a bond of confidence as a preliminary to a deep and lasting affection is more necessary, or better performed. In that situation the dog behaves as the eyes of the human. For sighted persons where dependence on the dog's cooperation is not so complete, the dog is used as a surrogate human, and as a prop to one's psyche. And if he is to perform that function completely he needs to be trained. And knowing dogs, Mr Tucker knows that dogs are naturally trainable and want to be trained, and to be loved. He has in this book provided us all with chapter and verse of how to train a dog, and placed in our hands a most valuable guide to better human experience.

D. C. Blood

Introduction

Although I have been with dogs since I was born, it was not until my early teens that my real interest in dog training began when I joined the Associated Sheep, Police and Army Dog Society. This paved the way for me to become a handler and instructor at the Royal Air Force Police Dog Training Centre where I learned much during my National Service. I then worked with the Guide Dogs for the Blind for the next twenty years, both in England and Australia. I do not think there are many people who can say that their work is also their hobby, but for me it has been and always will be.

It is amazing how something can start as a hobby and then become one's profession. I now have my own dog training school to which people bring their dogs for individual training. Special courses are also held for groups of people who are interested in more advanced obedience and tracking.

Many people have asked me why I have never written a book on dog training, and the only excuse I could give was that I found it hard to find the time. However, I realise that in the last few years the dog population has increased tremendously, and more and more people want to know and need to know how to select, manage, and train their dogs. Therefore I have set out to help people to do just that, by writing this book as simply as possible to cover the widest range of dog owners.

Basically it is written for the average dog owner. It is also written for those who want to progress to the more advanced stages of training, including those who want to train their dogs for the show ring or obedience trials. I hope that it will be well received by breeders, instructors, judges, stewards, and many others in the canine fraternity. I also hope that it will be of interest to members of the veterinary profession and to those who study any field of animal behaviour.

People who are interested in training their dogs for competitive work can, upon application, obtain the current rules and regulations from their respective Kennel Clubs, a list of which is given in the Appendix. These rules and regulations may be subject to alteration as they are revised from time to time. The Australian obedience trials rules are similar to those in the United States; the New Zealand and South African rules are similar to those in Great Britain.

The training methods explained in this book have either been taught to me by very experienced people, or been devised by myself. In all cases they have been used extensively and proven. Provided they are used correctly they should be very successful. But I would like to quote a saying which is often used in dog training circles: What one person can do by using certain training methods, another person may not necessarily achieve. Therefore, it is up to you to use the methods which give you the best results and which show that your dog really enjoys working with you.

Finally, I hope that when my readers have read this book they will have gained a better insight into their dogs' minds, and will, as a result, have a better understanding of the way they should best train their four-legged friends.

Michael Tucker

1

The Choice of Dog

Many people have problems with their dogs, and I find that in most cases this is either because they have not made the best selection when choosing a dog, or they have not known how to train him properly. While the majority of owners have dogs for companionship, more and more people are getting dogs for protection as well, and for this reason they tend to choose large dogs. In many cases it is the large dogs which become problem dogs; an owner often admits that as a puppy the dog was easy to handle, but as the dog grew stronger and larger he became unmanageable.

Because the owner could not control him on a leash when taking him for walks, it became easier to let him exercise himself in the back garden only. There he felt too enclosed and became frustrated. He would howl, bark, dig holes, pull the washing off the line, and do all sorts of naughty things. He soon became a nuisance to every one, and the family regretted buying him in the first place. This is a typical extreme case; others may be not so bad, but bad enough for owners to worry about.

I wonder how many people become disillusioned after owning a dog for a while, particularly when he becomes a nuisance and then grows up to be uncontrollable. A great many families decide to live with their uncontrolled dogs, either by keeping them shut up on their premises or letting them roam the streets all day; others seek advice on how to train them; while others again, assuming that alternative homes cannot be found for their dogs, completely shy away from their responsibilities and just dump their dogs somewhere instead of having them painlessly destroyed by a veterinary surgeon.

Nearly every day I receive a telephone call from a distressed dog owner who explains that his or her pet has now become completely out of hand. I am then asked if I can help the owner train it to become a well-behaved member of the family.

Except for a small minority who have reached the point of no return, most dogs can be trained to have their faults corrected. But I always point out, when making an appointment with the owner, that it is he or she who needs to be trained and not just the dog. Ideally the owners should receive instruction with their dogs once a week and, in addition to this, it is most important for them to train their dogs every day if progress is to be made and success is to be ultimately achieved.

By necessity (more than anything else) it is nearly always the wife who will bring the dog for training, because her husband is at work. Although it may look as if husbands expect their wives to do all the dog training, this is not always the case. It is the wife who is usually at home more with the dog than her husband is, and therefore she is in a better position to train the dog every day and at different times of the day. But it should not be left entirely to her, and I always welcome it when both husband and wife can attend a training session together with their dog. I know then that they are both interested in knowing how to carry out the training, and that they will both train their dog in the same way, thus ensuring that the dog will not be confused. A dog can easily be confused if one member of the family handles him in one way and another member handles him in a different way.

When an owner arrives at my Training School and gets her dog out of her car, the animal is often highly excited. It may whine, bark, jump up at her, pull very hard on the leash, and be generally out of control. Seeing the varied reactions of so many of these dogs, I never cease to wonder why on earth their owners ever chose such breeds in the first place. They pull their owners up my driveway, and anyone watching might well wonder if the owners were bringing their dogs for training or the dogs were taking their owners! As I said before, it is the owners who need the training, and all who take it up come to realise this in a very short time.

Some dogs are very bold and strong; others are very shy, mainly because their owners have not taken them out enough in their early puppy days so that they could get used to the outside world. Some become aggressive towards people and other animals because either the dogs have come from breeding stock possessing aggressive traits, or they have not been handled properly and corrected when the aggression first started. In a way the owners cannot be blamed every time. The point is that they have not known how to correct the dog in the first place.

My advice to people who want a dog is to give very careful consideration to the matter of which breed of dog they wish to have. They should not just look at a puppy as a lovely cuddly bundle of fluff with appealing little eyes, but they should first look at adult dogs of the same breed. This will give them a very good idea of what they can expect to be handling when the puppy is fully grown. They should then ask themselves, 'Will I be able to handle a dog of that size and strength, afford the cost of feeding him, and spend enough time exercising and training him every day and grooming his long coat if he has one?'

The next question to ask oneself is: 'For what purpose do I want a dog?' Consideration should be given to the sex of the dog one wishes to own. There are advantages and disadvantages for both sexes. In the case of a male dog, some owners may be looking ahead with the idea of owning a very good pedigree male for stud purposes, or just owning a dog which they can enter in the show ring or obedience trials all the year round. Generally speaking the male dog in any breed is more dominant than the female and therefore needs a firmer hand when he is being trained and handled.

Other people may wish to own a bitch with the idea of breeding from her. They have to accept the fact that she will be out of action for about three weeks every six months when she comes into season, and for longer when she is having puppies. The bitch is smaller in size than the male, and in most cases she proves to be more manageable and easier to train.

In Australia dogs and bitches have to be entire if one wishes to enter them in dog shows. The only exception to this rule is when a dog has been neutered in order to save its life. In this circumstance the owner must make written application to the member body of the Australian National Kennel Council, and such a dog is then normally permitted to compete in shows. In most States dogs and bitches which have been neutered for any reason are allowed to compete in obedience trials.

It would take too long to give a detailed list of all the breeds which have the working qualities which are considered ideal in the obedience trial working dog, but the breeds which are most adaptable to this kind of work are German Shepherds, Border Collies, Labrador Retrievers, Golden Retrievers, Irish Setters, Dobermann Pinschers, Weimaraners, Rottweilers, Poodles, Corgis, and Pointers, as well as Dalmatians, Great Danes, Boxers, Old English Sheepdogs, and Schnauzers; there are also a few others. It must be remembered that they all have their own individual characteristics and much depends on how the owners train them.

However, it is not everyone who wants to have a dog to enter in the shows and trials. Most people just want a dog as a pet and for company. They may happen to choose one of the breeds mentioned above, or they may choose any one of the spaniel or terrier families. They could decide to have one of the many hounds or a large, heavy breed such as the St Bernard, Newfoundland, Bullmastiff, or Pyrenean Mountain Dog. It may well be that they are not really interested in having a pedigree dog, but will be quite content to have a dog from the countless varieties of cross-breeds. While they usually know what breed the mother is, it is not always possible to know who the father was. This makes it difficult to guess how big the pup will be when he has finished growing. All these dogs can make good pets and, provided they are temperamentally sound, all are capable of at least responding to basic training. Beyond this, some will and some will not advance.

Generally speaking, the terrier types are bold little dogs with an instinct to hunt and kill small vermin, and so many of them will have a similar go at a stranger's ankles as he enters your premises! Members of the hound group have usually got their noses glued to the ground and, given the opportunity, will chase anything that moves and be quite oblivious to you calling them back. Spaniels are quite different. With their retrieving instinct they are easy to train and love working in the field. The large heavy breeds I have mentioned are very quick to learn and, although they may be slow plodding dogs, are very strong. If they ever get into a fight, you must be very careful, for your own sake, when trying to stop them. Owners who choose these enormous dogs should be quite sure in their own minds about their ability to control such animals.

One of the nicest breeds I have come across, particularly in Australia, is the Samoyed. Apart from it being a very attractive-looking dog, generally speaking its temperament is superb. In fact, I have rarely come across one which is not good. While they do not have a great capacity to learn beyond basic obedience, they are extremely friendly towards people and other dogs.

Other breeds, although they may look handsome in the show ring and may prove to be fairly good companions, can be very difficult even when being taught basic training. Being very independent types, they are just not adaptable to training like the working breeds are—they include Chow Chows, Borzois, Basenjis, Shih Tzus, Pekingese, Lhasa Apsos, and many of the lesser-known breeds.

Having decided upon the breed, you should enquire about proposed matings, or puppies that have been born. It is very important that you meet the sire and dam of the litter, for you can gain much by observing their temperaments, and this will give you a fairly good idea how their pups will develop. Examine the pedigrees carefully and make sure that everything on these forms is complete. All the facts can be checked by contacting the appropriate Kennel Council in each State.

It is worth taking the trouble to do all this because there are many 'back-yard' breeders operating today who will say that everything is in order, but who will not put it in writing, and they will often sell their stock for exorbitant prices.

It is pleasing to know that more and more people who want to buy a puppy now shop around looking at good breeding stock within the breed they fancy. However, they may then wonder what they should be looking for when they are ready to make their final choice among all the puppies. This is not an easy decision to make by any means, but if you watch the actions and reactions of puppies when you visit them, it will help you decide which one you should select.

Firstly, one should look for a bold, fit, happy, and alert puppy. You will see this as he comes up to meet you. Watch how he reacts to your voice and gentle handling, the way he licks your hand, and uses his nose. See how he gets on with all his litter mates and how he respects his mother. After a while move around and then, quietly at first, clap your hands. Observe how the pup follows you around and whether or not he dislikes the noise of your clapping hands. Do not worry if he seems to be a little mischievous—actually this is a good sign for it shows that he has a fair degree of initiative, something which is a great asset in a working dog. However, if there are signs of nervousness, or suspicion of strangers, or shyness to loud noises such as your hands clapping, then do not choose a puppy from that litter but look further afield for sound stock of your choice.

As mentioned above, many people have no desire to own a pedigree dog. All they want is a dog. To them it does not matter if it is pure bred or cross bred. They just want a pet and a companion. Some people acquire a dog from a private home, while others decide to take their pick from the local Lost Dog's Home. In a way I admire people who do this because most of them really want to give some poor unwanted dog a good home, but at the same time they really are taking a chance.

While the dog which they finally select may appear to be all right physically and temperamentally, he may not turn out to be this way after they have taken him home. There have been many cases where dogs have become sick with gastro enteritis. Far worse is the occasional case of distemper and within a few days such badly affected dogs have had to be destroyed. Often a dog, after settling into his new home, has shown bad temperamental traits even to the extent of being aggressive. It is quite likely that he was such a delinquent dog that his former owner just dumped him somewhere and eventually he was picked up and taken to the Lost Dogs' Home. Because he was not claimed he was put up for sale and, soon after settling into his new home, he reverted to being the local terror.

However, a lot of people do manage to get good dogs from these places; the animals settle down, train well, and become devoted pets.

Having made your choice, your immediate concern should be for the dog's health and upbringing. I therefore consider it to be very important to say a few words about your dog being inoculated against that dreadful disease, distemper. For those who are breeding, it is essential to give your bitch a booster inoculation just prior to mating or in the last two weeks of pregnancy. Providing she responds to this, she will be able to pass on this immunity to her pups through the milk they suckle from her. This natural immunity should keep them safe (although it cannot be guaranteed 100 per cent) until they are about eleven or twelve weeks of age, when they can receive their full inoculation against distemper and canine hepatitis. If the puppies are going to be placed in areas where there is a risk of such diseases, then additional protection can be given with a temporary vaccine at the age of six weeks. It is pleasing to note that a number of Lost Dogs' Homes are giving their dogs this inoculation, which virtually gives immediate immunity until they are ready to receive the full distemper-canine hepatitis inoculation.

Many veterinary surgeons advise people not to take their pups out until ten to fourteen days after they have had their inoculations at about twelve weeks of age.

However, many of us who train dogs believe in getting puppies used to the outside world, and we consider it to be necessary to take a puppy out for short walks on a leash a few days after he has settled into his new home, provided that he has received his temporary vaccine inoculation at six weeks and that you prevent him from coming into direct contact with stray dogs which may not have been inoculated, and also prevent him from sniffing around places where other dogs have been from which he could pick up a disease. If these precautions are taken, the chances of a puppy picking up a disease are very remote indeed.

The important thing about getting a puppy out and about as soon as possible is to introduce him gradually to as many things and people as possible in the early days of puppyhood. This is often referred to as puppy conditioning and it is the subject of Chapter 3. If the puppy is not taken out for walks until he is about fourteen weeks of age, then it is more than likely that he will show fear towards all sorts of things. I have come across many cases of this happening, and it is always a great pity.

So remember, get your puppy out consistently so that, apart from getting him well conditioned, you will also be getting him used to walking on the leash. But a word of warning: do not get over-enthusiastic and walk him too far, otherwise he will get exhausted. It is true that he needs some exercise, but he needs rest too as he grows up during puppyhood.

2

Dog Psychology and Puppy Training

Although many people do not realise it, there are some very critical periods in a puppy's life. The term 'critical period' can be defined as a time when a puppy's development can go one way or the other—for better or for worse, so to speak. It greatly depends on how you as the breeder or the owner rear him to give him that good start in life that he deserves.

From birth until he is about three weeks of age he is really dependent on his mother. The warmth, care, and food he gets from her are his only needs. In the next period, during his third or fourth week, a gradual change takes place. He starts to walk, respond to noises, eat solid food, and wag his tail. He plays with his litter mates and starts to explore. During this whole time it is important that he has the continued security of his mother, for at no other time in his life will emotional upsets (such as fear, brought about by sudden noises, being introduced to unfamiliar things, or being left alone) have a more harmful effect on him with more lasting results.

From about the fourth to the seventh week the pup will gradually wander further away from his mother to explore. He learns how to play with toys, recognise his master, respond to other voices, and meet other animals. Towards the end of this period is the best time for weaning, and the handing over to his new owners should occur ideally between the seventh and eighth week. Six weeks of age should be the absolute minimum for this and no pup should leave his mother before that age. On the other hand placing a puppy into his new home after the age of twelve weeks is not desirable either if you want to gain the best results. The reason for this is that the age of eight to twelve weeks is the most receptive time for the puppy to learn simple commands like 'Come', 'Sit', 'Heel', etc. He learns all these quite naturally and should not be forced to do them, or scolded, told off, or yelled at if he does not understand. You should try to mould the puppy into such a way of doing each exercise that he enjoys every moment to it. It then becomes habit.

As mentioned in the previous chapter, within a few days of a puppy's arrival at his new home, he should be gradually introduced to the things around him as he is taken out daily for very short walks on the leash.

16

Between the twelfth and the sixteenth week puppies often try to get their own way and a struggle starts between dog and owner, especially if the puppy has not had this earlier training. Now comes a time when a more serious type of training must be introduced so that the owner can gain the puppy's respect. He has to realise that the master is the boss and pack leader. If he steps out of line he will receive the necessary correction from his master, but will also be rewarded with sincere praise when he pleases his master.

From the fourth to the seventh month you should take the puppy even further afield to meet more people, other dogs and animals, and get him used to all sorts of things which happen in the street. Unless you continue to do this at this time of his life, you are likely to have a puppy fearful of things in the outside world, and very soon it will be too late to get him over those fears.

Of course this conditioning should not just stop at the age of seven months. It should go on throughout his entire puppyhood. When he becomes an adult at the age of twelve months he must still have his daily outings to prevent boredom and frustration.

At about the seventh to the ninth month a critical period affects dogs and bitches differently.

(a) The male puppy can really try to exercise his will over his owner, other people, and other animals. He may develop a protective attitude and show aggression. You have to be very firm when and if this happens, otherwise you will have a lot of trouble later on as he will rule over you.
(b) The bitch puppy can go through a difficult time as she experiences coming into season for the first occasion. You must make sure that she is not subjected to any form of stress or anxiety during this time, otherwise it could affect her temperament.

From the ninth to the twelfth month both male and female puppies continue to adjust as they come into full adulthood, and you can expect to see fluctuations in their temperament, training ability, and working performance.

The times of these critical periods are only approximate and they vary from breed to breed and from dog to dog. All we have to do is to be aware of them and manage our dogs accordingly as they go through puppyhood.

Upon reaching adulthood all dogs gradually go into the stage known as the age of maturity. It can be described as an age when dogs become quite settled in temperament, can absorb more advanced forms of training, and are steadier in their working ability.

For example, the Labrador Retriever is considered to be the breed which matures the earliest, and that is why it can be trained as a guide dog for the blind at the age of twelve months. In contrast, the German Shepherd (which in my opinion makes the best guide dog, provided he has a capable owner) does not mature until he is at least eighteen months, and that is why guide dog training centres throughout the world prefer not to train this breed until it is mature enough to absorb this very demanding and exacting type of work. Other well-known breeds which are also trained as guide dogs are: Boxers (which mature at about sixteen months), Golden Retrievers (at eighteen months) and Border Collies (at two years).

Further up the scale, Dobermann Pinschers (which incidently are not suitable for guide dog work) mature at about three years, as do many other breeds. So, although all dogs can be trained to perform simple basic obedience exercises, advanced and demanding work should be given only when the dog is mature and ready for it. It is well to remember, therefore, not to push along too fast with your dog's training, otherwise he could crack up under the strain, and so could you! Instead, you should train steadily so that the dog's mental capacity can cope with everything you teach him.

Training a dog is not just a matter of giving a whole lot of commands and jerks on the leash; you have to look right into a dog's mind and find out how it ticks. You can gain much knowledge on the subject just by living closely with the animal. You get to know him, and he gets to know you. Some people have a natural ability to 'read' a dog's mind. Factors involved include learning about the characteristics of different breeds, observing their instinctive behaviour and reactions, being able to anticipate their movements, and accepting the fluctuations which occur from day to day in any dog's performance.

The domesticated dog still retains much of its pack instinct and, in its own way, reads his masters moods and actions to a very fine degree. People often refer to a dog or breed as being highly intelligent. It would be better to say that the dog has an extensive capacity to learn and possesses great instinctive powers. The word 'intelligent' should, I believe, be applied to the human race only. We know that $6 \times 7 = 42$ and can work out a great many things in mathematics and other subjects, but a dog cannot. However, he has an inborn instinct and he uses his senses in an amazing way which I will talk about later.

When you collect your new puppy from the breeder and bring him home it will be the first upheaval he has experienced. He has been taken away from his first home, his mother, and perhaps other members of the litter.

He now comes into completely strange surroundings with new smells and possibly a different climate. Let him settle in in his own time. Firstly, it is a good idea to put him in the back garden, which should be totally enclosed. Most puppies are quite inquisitive and immediately use their noses to explore new territory. It is important that you stay with your puppy to give him confidence. Talk to him, walk around with him and try to make him feel happy. Watch him carefully, for it is possible that he will relieve himself, whereupon you can praise him sincerely by saying 'Good dog' as soon as he has had a little wee. When he has made a thorough examination of the back garden, which should be free of anything upon which he could harm himself, he should then be invited into the house where he can carry out a further exploration.

We all have to face up to the fact that we are going to have natural accidents with our young puppies when they relieve themselves in the house. All too often an owner immediately chastises a puppy by shouting at him and hitting him, or by using a rolled up newspaper on him, or even by rubbing his nose in the mess.

These forms of punishment should never be given. They often make the dog worse, and he will continue to mess in a state of anxiety. This then becomes a regular occurrence and finally the owner decides never to have the dog inside again, because he is dirty. I always think it is a pity when an owner does not allow his dog into the home. If the dog is allowed inside, owner and dog will form a closer bond of companionship than would otherwise be possible and the owner will have increased opportunity to study, train, and generally get to know his dog.

But let us look deeper into the puppy's mind in connection with his messing on your best carpet. From the time that he was born he carried out this natural function in the nest and the kennel, and who cleaned it up? That's right—his mother. It was a natural habit for him to do it there, and now when you bring the puppy into new surroundings your best carpet may well seem like the nest in which he was born. You will notice that I used the term 'natural habit'. What we have to do now is to teach the puppy a new habit, by taking him at regular intervals to a particular part of the back garden and by repeatedly using a term such as 'Busy! Busy!' (in a quiet drawn-out tone of voice). As soon as he has performed, he should be praised with kindly-spoken words like 'Good boy'. When he does do it in the house, a firm 'No' is all that is necessary, and immediately take him outside to his toilet ground and repeat the word 'Busy'. To safeguard the puppy messing in the house it is up to us, as owners, to put the puppy outside regularly. It will then become such a habit in the back garden that he will not want to do it inside.

Later, and in fact for the rest of the dog's life, the word 'Busy' will be very useful, as it can be used in other suitable places away from home, and the dog will perform even to the extent of trying although he may have nothing to pass.

By far the quickest and surest way of getting to know any dog is by feeding him. Out of the three meals a day that he is to have, one will contain meat cut into small pieces. Take one of these pieces from the plate of food which you have placed on a table and out of his reach, rub it firmly on to the palm of your hand, and then hand feed it to him. As he takes the meat and licks the meat juice off your fingers he will be taking in your natural scent, and thus a natural bond will be formed between dog and master.

Having whetted his appetite, take another piece of meat as before in the right hand and, walking backwards and drawing your hand towards you and between your legs, say quietly and enthusiastically 'Prince, come'. He should immediately respond by running straight towards you. As he does, you should go on praising him, saying in a pleasant tone as if you really mean it, 'Good dog. Clever dog'. This exercise of teaching him to come is known as the recall and will soon become a great game with your dog and one which he will enjoy immensely (fig. 1).

The recall is the most important exercise in dog training. It is gratifying to know that you can teach this to a young puppy, and you will find that during this exercise five very important things will be happening.

1. The bond between dog and master continues to be fostered.
2. The puppy is learning his name.
3. He is learning the word 'Come'.
4. The formation of the straight line recall is being established.
5. He links the sincere praise with the meat reward.

It is interesting to note that these five things have resulted from your training the puppy on two natural lines: (a) the means of survival—food, and (b) the puppy using his number one sense—the sense of smell.

The next day, having introduced the initial step of the recall, you can then start to build on it. As your puppy comes to your feet to take the meat held between

Above: Fig. 1. 'Prince, come!' The puppy comes for the meat held in the right hand. *Below:* Fig. 2. The right hand is drawn in and raised a little; the command 'Sit' is given, and the puppy's hindquarters are pushed down gently and towards his front paws as he takes the meat

your finger and thumb of your right hand, raise your hand up between your knees so that he will lift his head a little to nibble the meat. At this point, quietly but quickly command him to 'Sit', and carefully push his rear end down and towards you with your left hand, fingers and thumb being spread out to fit around his hindquarters in a semi-circular fashion (fig. 2). You should have no trouble in this; he will be relaxed because he is interested in eating the meat. Praise him each time he does it. He needs to have this training about half a dozen times at one of the feeding times each day and, when the training is over, he can eat the rest of the food out of his bowl.

You should find that after about three more days of coming and sitting he will sit automatically in front of your feet (fig. 3). From there, you can now teach him to come around the back of your legs and sit at your left side in the heel position. This is known as the 'Finish to the Recall'.

After carrying out two or three simple recalls, take up two pieces of meat in your right hand. Recall him again and, when he sits in front of you, reward him with one piece of meat. Then quietly say 'Heel' and entice him to follow the second piece of meat held in your right hand around and close behind your right leg (fig. 4). Transfer the meat to your left hand behind you and get him to continue to follow around the back of your left leg to your left side. At this point transfer the meat again to your right hand, lift it a little so that he has to raise his head, command him to 'Sit', and carefully push his hindquarters down with your left hand (fig. 5). Then praise as usual and feed him the piece of meat (fig. 6). He has now learned how to walk around the back of you and sit close and straight beside your left foot.

After a few more days you can build a

Above: Fig. 3. Later he will come and sit automatically and the meat is replaced with sincere praise. *Below:* Fig. 4. The command 'Heel' is given and the puppy is enticed with the meat to walk around your back and to your left side

Left: Fig. 5. The meat is transferred back into the right hand and held just above the puppy's nose as he arrives at your side and is commanded to 'Sit', his hindquarters being pushed carefully down and forwards.
Right: Fig. 6. The puppy is praised gently as he takes the meat

little more. Having completed two or three recalls with a finish to the heel position, say 'Heel' and, holding a piece of meat in the right hand just in front of his nose, walk forward a few steps. As you do so he will follow; say 'Sit' and come to a halt, pushing his hindquarters down gently with your left hand, and feed him the meat with praise. This short exercise just gives him a little insight into walking at heel beside you.

You are now really building as you go and these are exercises which do not drain his mental powers; in fact he enjoys doing them. But now you do not need to keep pacing up and down the back lawn, or on the kitchen floor if you decide to do it indoors, you can do it all from one position. When you have called him on the first recall and brought him around to heel, take another piece of meat off the plate (which is on top of the table within your arm's reach). Show the puppy the piece of meat, throw it a few metres in front of you, and say 'Fetch'. He should immediately rush after it and eat it. As he does so, praise him, take some meat from the plate, recall him to you, and do a finish. This you could do half a dozen times, and then end up with him heeling beside you for a couple of metres.

As you can see, not only does this stage of puppy training allow you to remain in one position, but it is also allowing the puppy to use his initiative to leave you to pursue the food several times. The entire exercise will become a pattern in his mind.

This method of teaching the recall to a very young puppy should only be used to form a foundation of the exercise in the puppy's mind. Ideally, it should be used only at one of his three meals per day, and it should be completely phased out by the end of three weeks. During all this time you should at other times of the day put in the odd recall without using meat. Of course the meat reward is replaced by sincere vocal and physical praise. I find it best to use the meat every day for the first ten days, and over the next twelve days gradually to phase it out by using it once every two days, once every three days, and so on.

Do not make the mistake of using the meat at more than one session a day or for several weeks and then drop it off altogether. If you do this, you are likely to end up with the puppy coming only when you have food and at no other time. So remember, it is a method which can be used to lay the foundation only and just for very young puppies. It is not wise to use it with older puppies or adult dogs, as you will find that they will come only for food and nothing else. They are old enough to have the more serious type of training which you will find in Chapter 11.

You can also teach the puppy to stand and lie down. The most convenient time of the day to teach a puppy to stand is when you are grooming him on a table. If he sits while you are brushing him, gently place

Fig. 7. To teach the puppy to stand, hold his front with your right hand, give him the command 'Stand', and lift him up gently with your left hand, and praise

your hand under his belly, say slowly and gently, 'Stand', gently lift him up, and praise him. If you do this every time he sits or lies down, in time he will gradually learn the meaning of the word 'Stand' (fig. 7).

When teaching your puppy to lie down, choose a time in the evening when he is not too energetic and excitable. Sit him on the lawn or a piece of carpet on your left side; for your own convenience you can kneel on the floor. Place your left hand on

23

Left: Fig. 8. With your left hand on his shoulders, command 'Drop' or 'Down' and lift his paws up with your right hand. *Right:* Fig. 9. Praise him under the chin with your right hand

his shoulders, take his right foreleg at the knee joint between the thumb and first finger of your right hand. Pick up the leg, take it over to his left foreleg and take hold of that at the knee joint between your first and second fingers. Say 'Drop' or 'Down', lift both legs up under his chin, and at the same time push his shoulders down with your left hand (fig. 8). As soon as he is lying down, praise him with your voice and stroke him slowly and gently under his chin with your right hand. Your left hand should rest lightly on his shoulders (fig. 9).

Keep him there for about five to ten seconds and no longer. Then say 'Go free', and allow him to go away and play. Try the exercise once more during the evening and only for a few seconds. This will gradually prepare him for more serious training later on. You will find this method easy to use for all puppies, no matter what size or breed. However, it is not so easy to use when training an adult dog belonging to a large breed, and therefore other methods have to be used which are explained in Chapter 13.

3
Puppy Conditioning

Apart from giving a puppy a good home, nourishing food, and much love and consideration, the most important aspect which any dog owner should give special attention to is conditioning the dog to everything in the world around him.

Let us first take a look at how a dog sees the family in the home, and some of the daily activities. A puppy enjoys the company of human beings and being fed and generally cared for by them, but from time to time unpleasant incidents can happen in the home. These can be so startling to the puppy that he will continue to fear and avoid them for the rest of his life.

Imagine that he is asleep on the carpet, and a vacuum cleaner near him is suddenly switched on. This can have a terrifying effect on him, and from then on he will probably crouch in a corner every time the machine is brought out for use. There are many other things which could frighten him, such as being knocked by a broom head as you sweep the floor, or being knocked by the leg of a chair as you push it back in haste. In fact there are scores of incidents like these that could happen and it would be very unfortunate if your dog

was frightened by such things all because you did not think carefully and find out where the puppy was in the first place. What you need to do, therefore, is to stoop down to his height and find out how he sees everything happening at his eye level. By doing this you can gain a deeper understanding of his feelings and the reasons why he can become frightened.

With such things as vacuum cleaners and appliances you use daily it is best to switch them on when the puppy is well away from them, so that he can hear them start and make a gradual approach to them. But it is also important that you should be there to support him with your voice, encouraging and inviting him to come and have a look at what you are doing.

Let us take a look at how he meets people who come into your home. Imagine, for instance, that a friend of yours has called; you invite him in to sit down in a comfortable chair and have a friendly chat. It may well be that he is a big man who talks with a loud voice and has a genuine love for animals, even though he may not know the correct way to approach them or handle them. It so happens that you have not mentioned to him that you have recently acquired a puppy, and before you realise it the dog trots into the room. Your friend, being delighted to see that you have a puppy, jumps up from his chair, walks across the room, and swoops down with his large hands to pick up your puppy. The dog could be terrified as this strange person seems like a giant as he rises from his chair and thumps across the room and his huge hands descend like grabs from a crane! Is it any wonder that the puppy becomes frightened of people? Not only will he always associate your particular friend with a very unpleasant experience, but he may think that everyone who comes into your home from that day on is going to descend on him in the same way.

You must therefore take all necessary precautions to safeguard anything going wrong like this. A much better procedure would be for you to have the puppy outside or in another room; then invite your friend to sit down, tell him that you have a new puppy, and ask him to remain seated while you call the puppy into the room. Also ask your friend to wait until the puppy has approached him and request that he talks to the puppy quietly and then slowly lowers his hand to the puppy. This gives the puppy time and room to meet your friend. The puppy's confidence will grow to such an extent that he will accept all people coming into your house as good people in whom he can trust and to whom he can show affection.

A puppy's conditioning is not just in the house, but also in the back garden. This should be totally enclosed to prevent him from escaping, but at the same time there should be a section of the fencing through which he can see. Puppies who are enclosed by high brick walls or close-boarded fencing often become suspicious and nervous of strange noises which they hear but cannot see the cause of on the other side of their enclosure. Some of the best guide dog training establishments in the world, which breed their own stock, ensure that their puppy enclosures are made of cyclone fencing from the ground upwards and are situated at places where there is regular daily activity, so that the puppies can see as well as hear all that goes on around them. It is essential that these puppies are fully conditioned to everything in life in which they are going to lead and care for their future owners who are blind.

Some properties are enclosed by a combination of walls, close-boarded fencing, and other fencing through which dogs can see. The latter may be situated on the side of a thoroughfare or passageway along which pedestrians can walk. In these circumstances there is a high risk that children, and indeed some adults, will tease the dog through the fence. This will annoy and frustrate the dog to such a degree that he will become aggressive to people passing by and then to people you invite on to your premises. You should make sure that this does not happen to your puppy, even if it means keeping him within an inner fence near your house.

A puppy should be fitted with a small leather collar as soon as he enters his new home. It does not take long for him to become used to wearing it, and within a day or two you should also get him used to walking around the back garden on a long leather leash. This should be light in weight but strong, and it should have a good clip on it. Again it does not take long for the puppy to become accustomed to walking on a leash, but if it is somewhat apprehensive of it, you can try clipping it on and letting him trail it around for a few minutes under your supervision, to ensure that the leash does not become caught in anything or that the puppy does not decide to chew it up.

The next step is to take him for a short walk in your local neighbourhood. He is now venturing into the outside world and he needs all the praise and encouragement you can give him. It is not necessary to keep him on your left side all the time, but let him move all around you on the leash as you walk along.

It is most important that you always have a long leash—about 120 cm in length. The reason for this is that when a puppy sees a strange object or hears an odd noise he may well show fear and his natural reaction is to escape. If this happens and you have a short leash or indeed a tight one, his fear will increase because he will feel like a prisoner and be unable to get away. But with a long leash he can move around more freely, especially if the handler moves with him and talks to him in a way that will calm him down and restore his confidence. The large area in which he can revolve around the handler at the end of a leash is known as the 'Dog's Area of Independence'.

A 120-cm leash does not have to be used all the time. You may wish to have it shorter. It is best therefore always to hold the handle of the leash in the right hand, and also grip it at a second point a little further down using the thumb and first finger of the right hand. If and when the puppy is frightened for some reason or another, that second point down the leash can be released instantly so that the puppy can move away and not feel so restricted. Your left hand should be used only for correcting the puppy on the leash, which I will explain in more detail later in this book.

There are many things on the streets which appear to be very strange to a young puppy, and consequently he can be suspicious of them. All dogs, without exception, show suspicion of something at some time in their lives. Although it is a natural trait, you have to help your puppy overcome these daily suspicions and this is all part of his temperamental conditioning.

Suppose that when walking along a footpath your puppy sees a green garbage bag billowing slightly in the breeze, or some other equally alarming object; he shows fear and dashes away from it to a safe distance. Having allowed him to move away anything up to the fullest extent of the leash, in which case it may be necessary to change the leash from one hand to the other, you then have to coax him up to the object (fig. 10).

Of course it is no good pulling the puppy towards it and saying something like 'Come here; it won't hurt you'. If you did this, it would probably alarm the dog more and then he would be afraid of all sorts of strange objects. Instead you can work on the dog's natural curiosity. Keeping the puppy on a long leash, go up to the object yourself and examine it slowly and quietly, and at the same time encourage and praise the puppy vocally (fig. 11). In this way you can draw the interest out of him. He will come to feel that he is missing out on something, something which his master is enjoying. Slowly but surely he should advance towards the object until he sniffs it (fig. 12). At this point you should give more quiet praise to build up his confidence (fig. 13). Not only does he build up confidence in himself but also in you. The puppy should be given plenty of time to carry out a thorough examination of the object. This may take some time and you must be very patient. When the puppy has completely satisfied himself that nothing is going to hurt him, you should take him

Above: Fig. 10. Dog (in this case a bitch) shows suspicion towards a strange object and retreats. *Below:* Fig. 11. Still suspicious, she crawls to investigate

Above: Fig. 12. She builds up confidence to make contact with the toy pig, sniffs it thoroughly, and realises it is not alive. *Below:* Fig. 13. Suspicion overcome, she is now quite happy

back a few metres to make another casual approach to the object, praising him all the time. In nearly every case when the puppy passes it a second time, he will show no suspicion.

I think the funniest occasion I have ever experienced in this respect was years ago when I was in the final stages of training a male Labrador to be a guide dog. He was leading me through the book section of a large Melbourne department store. Suddenly he gave a little bark and moved backwards. I instantly released his guide dog harness from my left hand and allowed him to go back to the full extent of the leash. I then stooped to see what had made him suddenly suspicious. Immediately I saw what it was. A female shop assistant was dusting the books with a feather duster. When he noticed her she had her back to him, was crouched straightening some books on the bottom shelf, and had put the duster under her arm. With her green overall just touching the floor, and her head, hands, and feet obscured from view, she appeared to him to be some strange green animal with a feathered tail! Naturally I had to do something about this, so I approached the lady, who was now standing up, explained the situation, and asked her help. Seeing the funny side of it, she was most willing to cooperate. We let the dog examine the feather duster; he wagged his tail and was very happy to meet the lady. I then asked her to re-enact the situation at which he earlier had shown suspicion. This she did. I took him back a few metres and then towards her. As he passed her he wagged his tail again, having completely overcome his suspicion. I thanked the lady for her cooperation, and ever since then she has looked back on the incident as one of the highlights of her work in the store.

Apart from conditioning your puppy to

various things on the streets you must also get him used to being handled by men, women, and children of all heights.

A great number of pedestrians admire the sight of a puppy on a leash and will often ask, 'How old is he? What is his name?' and if uncertain will ask, 'What breed is he?' I always believe it is an opportunity not to be missed when answering their questions, to invite the puppy up to the people and ask them if they would mind stroking him gently after he has sniffed their hands and accepted them. It is quite possible that you will meet many of the same local people from day to day; as you approach them with your puppy, greet them by saying 'Hello!' and then say to your puppy 'Come along and meet them', and as he does so praise him by saying 'Good boy'. Your praise will support him and help to give him confidence in going up to people (fig. 14).

Fig. 14. All puppies should be conditioned to meeting people in the street

It is also interesting to note that he will even start to respond when he hears you use the word 'Hello' for he will associate it with meeting people. From time to time I have demonstrated this point when I am out for a walk with my dog. I carry on some conversation with myself and suddenly mention the word 'hello' in my speech. My dog immediately shows great alertness and curiosity as she looks around in all directions to see who it is that I have greeted! It is quite amusing to watch and if she could talk she would probably say, 'Who on earth is it that you have met, and where are they?' This shows quite clearly how a dog will respond to sounds such as single words or short phrases. It all depends on how we say them and how often we use them in order to get that response from the dog.

The noise and sight of traffic is another thing to which you must gradually condition your puppy. When walking a young puppy it is not a good thing to go near busy traffic at first, but let him meet very light traffic which he can view from a distance and so build up confidence in himself. It is a good idea to select a place several metres away from the main road, where you can stay for a while. Here your puppy can observe traffic of all shapes, sizes, and noises. Again you should talk to him quietly to keep him calm and steady. But imagine how the puppy would view the traffic if you stood with him close to the kerb side. All traffic would look enormous and at the angle from which he looks up from the ground, traffic would be towering over him to a terrifying degree. Now it may well happen that all traffic has been halted and you intend to cross over the road with your puppy. This is good for him to walk with you among the vehicles where engines are quietly ticking over, but avoid at all costs ever taking your puppy near the exhaust pipes of such vehicles. Apart from the fumes being poisonous, they will make the puppy afraid of walking through such conditions again.

In extremely cold climates such as occur in England, exhaust fumes can remain in the air for several seconds after a car has moved away from a stationary position where its engine has been running, and a dog will be very reluctant to walk across the road until the fumes have dispersed.

One of the biggest problems we have on our roads these days is the large number of stray and unwanted dogs roaming around, and one of the most common faults of dogs which are on leashes is that they are very distracted by and sometimes even aggressive towards these stray dogs.

The main reason for this dog distraction is lack of dog socialisation when the dog was young. Naturally every dog likes to meet one of his own species. Here we can select and make use of many of the stray dogs on our streets. Many dog owners who take their dogs out on the streets and see another dog coming hold on very tightly to their own dog, often winding the leash around their hand so many times that there is no more leash left to wind. Their dog's area of independence has been greatly reduced; his front feet are hardly touching the ground; he feels like a prisoner and is then confronted with this unknown quantity of a rat-bag of a stray who is completely unrestricted. The hackles on the owner's dog rise, giving an indication of caution, and out of sheer fear he shows aggression in order to protect himself. The stray dog naturally retaliates and the battle is on. This is the most common cause of dog distraction and animal aggression and these traits often become progressively worse.

When clients come to me to receive basic

training with their young dogs, I always show them how to socialise their dogs with the strays, most of whom are well known to me in my local area, and I refer to them as my 'unpaid assistants'. Most of the strays will come at my request, do a good job in meeting the dog I have on the leash, and then go home when I have decided that I have had enough of them, often to the amusement of my client who is standing by!

Even if you are walking your young pup at heel when a stray dog or another dog on a leash approaches, it is best to break off from training your dog to walk at heel and prepare to socialise your dog. Use words like 'Go free' or 'Go on then' so that in time he will understand that he can leave the heel position. Hold the handle of the leash, keep it slack, but at the same time hold it high so that the dog will not accidently step over it and get tied up. Talk very slowly and quietly to your dog, using praising words. This type of talking will not only support your dog, but will often have a calming effect on the other dog as well. (fig. 15). When dogs meet like this, they will usually walk around each other and it is very important that you move around as well so that the other dog is

Fig. 15. Dogs being introduced on the leash for the first time

always on the opposite side and not between you and your dog. There are two reasons for this: firstly, you are always in an ideal position to pull your dog away in the event of a fight, and secondly, your dog, if he has reached a mature age, may tend to protect you if he realises that the other dog stands between you and him. Do not stand too near or give any physical praise by touching either of them. If you touch the other dog, yours might become jealous; if you touch yours, he may become protective for you. You should never bend down to your dog because this will also promote protective aggression, and you should never shout or talk loudly as it may excite and stir the dogs to have a fight.

During this meeting on the street, read your own dog carefully and observe the other dog at the same time.

A dog can indicate his feelings of cautiousness in many ways. His approach can be slow and sometimes the body crouches a little. Upon reaching the other dog he will hold himself up, his legs will become somewhat stiff, and he will virtually tiptoe slowly around the other dog. The coat on his back and sometimes on his tail will become erect. He will arch his neck and the tail may come up high, giving short quivering wags. While his head hardly moves, his eyes, having a glassy expression, will roll sideways towards the other dog. A dog will sometimes make a vocal expression such as a very slow growl. When dogs meet they will sniff at particular parts of each other where scent glands activate (figs 16 and 17), but more about this in Chapter 6 where I discuss the dog's senses.

Always give dogs time to settle and try to keep calm yourself. If you tense up and worry, you will convey this to the dogs by means of scent which you excrete, and dogs have an uncanny way of detecting this.

You can do much by using a calm slow quiet voice when your dog meets another. Gradually you will see him relax. His legs

Left: Fig. 16. The submissive one sits as the dominant one sniffs her neck. *Right:* Fig. 17. The dominant one stands still as the other one sniffs her neck

32

will move more freely, the fur on his back will lower, and his tail will fall to a lower level and give relaxed happy wags. He will have a happier look in his eyes and he will carry his neck and head in a relaxed posture. His quiet growling should either stop or gradually turn into an interested whine, and his whole attitude should change into one of wanting to invite the other dog to play (fig. 18).

As soon as you consider your dog has become settled with the other dog, command him to heel and walk on down the footpath. As time goes on he will accept all dogs as being normal and become so used to them being on the street that eventually he will virtually ignore them all, especially when he is walking at heel.

Perhaps the best examples seen of well-conditioned puppies are those youngsters bred to be guide dogs for the blind. They are well reared and walked by people who put a tremendous amount of time into conditioning and socialising them to everything in life. When they reach the age of maturity they are taken to guide dog training centres where they undergo their complete guide dog training. Dogs for this

Fig. 18. A good relationship is made—'Let's play!'

demanding work must be very sound in temperament to be trained to lead their sightless owners through every situation imaginable. This is the goal we should all aim for when rearing all our puppies, regardless of what the purpose is for which we are raising them.

4
Common Problems

How often have you heard a dog owner say, 'I have a problem dog! He wrecks everything at home, he barks and howls all day, I can't stop him jumping up, he steals food, I can't take him out for a walk as he wears me out pulling on the leash, I just can't do a thing with him, he can't be trusted!'

Now this sort of story is pretty sad, and yet it is far more likely that it is the owner who is the problem rather than the dog. There are many reasons for this. The owner obviously does not understand the dog, he has not conditioned and trained it properly, he has possibly left the dog on its own for hours on end, and when he has come home he has not given it the attention it deserves.

There are, however, other owners who have provided all these things for their dogs and yet they still have problems. In cases like these a frequent cause is that there is some form of tension in the owner or within the family. This cause seems to be on the increase as the pace of life increases. People have all sorts of nervous tensions resulting from overwork, business pressure, anxiety, family discord, and many other causes. Although most people do not

realise it, their dogs, being inwardly sensitive, can detect these human tensions and they respond to them in extraordinary ways.

When you have a problem with your dog you should objectively try to work out what caused it in the first place. Whatever it is, it is unacceptable to you, but as far as he is concerned he thinks it is great fun to do it. He enjoys doing it; he likes to have his own way, and his natural instincts, numerous as they are, are seen time and time again. Of all these, his instinct of self-preservation is paramount.

Take the case of a dog who jumps up at people. For the dog it is one way of expressing his joy at meeting someone. It becomes a problem to us when our clothes are ruined by his muddy paws or when he knocks the children over by his weight and force.

There are two ways of stopping a dog jumping up. As you approach your dog or as he approaches you anticipate that he will jump up at you. Give a command like 'Off'; lean slightly forward with your right hand clenched and held out a little from the centre of your body so that he hits his head on your hand as he jumps up. You will need to position your hand very carefully for this correction. Be careful not to raise your hand or bring it close to your body, otherwise he will be able to run up the front of you. You will notice that it will be an unpleasant sensation for the dog when he hits his head against your hand. It would be quite wrong for you to hit him on the head with your hand. This would make him hand shy and he would then be afraid to come when called.

The second method can be used with the aid of the leash and collar. Imagine he jumps up at people when they come to your house. Before they enter put him on the leash and as they approach say to him 'Off'. He will almost certainly jump up at them, whereupon you must jerk him down instantly. Then ask the people to retreat a few paces in order to make another approach; repeat the same command 'Off', and give a downward jerk on the leash if necessary. Repeat this until he obeys the command, and then quietly praise him for obeying. Always remember that your leash and collar are your equipment of control. They are the two essential items used in dog training. Later you will be able to control your dog with your voice and perhaps a hand signal if you consider it necessary. Much later on you will not even need to say 'Off'. Your dog will know that he must not jump up, and by your persistent training, you will have prevented this habit from developing.

There are two other methods of correction which I am very much against. They appear in a number of books on dogs and I strongly advise people not to use them. One is where you hit the dog with a rolled up newspaper. This method is used for correcting all sorts of problems. It can make a dog afraid when he sees someone holding a paper or magazine, and it can make some of the bolder types of dogs aggressive and if this happens it is disastrous. The other method is to knee the dog in the chest as it jumps up at you. This can be very dangerous to the dog. I saw this done once, the person having followed the instructions she had read in a book, and the dog collapsed in a heap on the ground. Fortunately I managed to revive it with some gentle massage and I strongly advised the owner never to do it again.

Many dog owners have a problem with their dogs pulling the washing off the clothes line. Now all young dogs want to play with things and, although most of them are given toys to play with such as an old shoe or ball, they love to chew more valued possessions, especially ones that move like the washing on the line.

There is a well-known principle in dog training which states that when training a dog you should always be in a position to prevent or correct any wrong move the dog may make.

When you hang the washing on the line have the dog with you so that, if he decides to grab it, you can correct him. Do not leave him in the garden unattended and, if you have to go indoors, make sure that you can watch him from a window. If you cannot be there to watch and correct him, either remove the dog from the garden or remove the washing from the line. It is as simple as that, and yet people will leave their dogs outside while they go shopping, only to return a few hours later and find their washing torn to shreds. For this some owners lose their tempers and punish their dogs with a beating. They will achieve no good by doing this. A dog certainly will not have the slightest idea that it was for having a swinging time on the washing line half an hour before and he will probably cower every time his owner returns. The above situation is a good illustration of the principle that if you really want to train your dog properly, you must be in a good position to do something about it. The same sort of procedure applies for dogs who dig holes, pull up shrubs, chew the furniture or the childrens' toys, and commit other similar crimes.

When your dog is left out in the open for a long time he can get bored and frustrated. He may resort to non-stop barking and howling, which is annoying to the neighbours, to say the least. The next thing you know is that you will have a visit from the local council inspector to say that he has received complaints about your noisy dog.

What has happened is that, being outside, your dog has barked when things have disturbed him and there was no one there to stop him. If this goes on and on it becomes a habit. With this type of problem it is best to keep your dog in a suitable place indoors and, if you have to keep him inside for several hours, make sure that you take him out for a good walk first thing in the morning and then again in the evening.

With the exception of the Basenji, which does not bark, and the Husky, which rarely barks but howls instead, all dogs bark to a greater or lesser extent. It is one of their ways of communicating with one another. Some people think that dogs communicate with humans, particularly their owners, by barking, but this is not necessarily so. When a dog barks he expresses his feelings at that time and, depending on how well you know him, you can interpret his feelings. I shall say more about this in a later chapter, but while a little barking is acceptable, anything more than this should be discouraged. Usually a firm command like 'Quiet', followed immediately with a firm upward jerk on the leash will be enough to stop your dog barking. However, if he persists, you can correct him in another way.

Take hold of your dog by the scruff of the neck with both hands, look him straight in the eye, say 'Quiet', give him two or three quick but firm shakes, and let go (fig. 19). This has an amazing effect on the dog and, provided you do it firmly, he should respond. The reason for this is that he accepts this type of physical correction instinctively. Remember when he was a puppy? Whenever he stepped out of line his mother used to pick him up by the scruff of his neck in her mouth and give him a quick shake. Remember how he respected her immediately? So if we do the same thing he will respect us. Another good thing about this type of correction is that he will never hold it against us, and this is important if we wish to have his respect and affection.

While most dogs, particularly young ones, are very energetic, it is very important that they be given time to sleep and rest without being disturbed. If they are disturbed, they become tired, irritable, and then bad tempered.

Sleeping quarters, especially at night time, should be free from flies and mosquitoes. Such irritating insects can make life intolerable for dogs. Grooming a dog before he goes to bed at night will help to make him feel comfortable. A dog whose coat is full of dead fur and dirt will naturally want to scratch. Scratching becomes a habit and, apart from being annoying to watch, can lead to a variety of skin troubles. Fleas

Right: Fig. 19. A physical correction which the dog understands instinctively. Take hold of him, look him straight in the eyes, give a corrective word and a few firm shakes. He will respect you and never hold it against you

on a dog are enough to send him around the bend, so when you see him having a real bout of scratching, check his coat thoroughly to see if he has picked up any fleas. Then get to work immediately by giving him a bath in any of the solutions designed to get rid of them. If it appears to be some type of skin irritation, do not hesitate to consult a veterinary surgeon.

As well as keeping your dog clean whenever you see him scratching or biting himself, give him a command like 'Stop scratching' and immediately stop him with your hand on his leg. If you consistently prevent and correct this bad habit by saying something like 'No scratching' and by physically stopping him scratching with your hand, you will eventually be able to stop him on command alone. In fact, if you are very quick in reading your dog's intentions, you should be able to give this command as a prevention before his claws get in the first scratch.

We had a saying in the Royal Air Force Police Dog Training Centre that 'grooming time is inspection time'. How true this is! It soon became a motto when we lectured on the health and care of our dogs.

Another every-day problem people have with their dogs is in connection with feeding them bones. Many dogs become very protective over their bones, far more protective, in fact, than they are over an ordinary bowl of dog food. The reason for this probably goes back to the days when dogs lived in a wild state, when they hunted and killed other animals and lived off their carcasses. Personally, I do not believe a dog should have too many bones, but the occasional one is all right. A good, raw, meaty beef shank bone is something he can really chew on to bring his teeth through and exercise his jaws. He can rip the meat off it and get out the marrow, which is good for him, but too many bones can give him constipation and cause him much discomfort.

Giving a dog bones can also promote protective aggression. When you feed a bone to your dog it is best that he should have it on his own, say in the laundry. It is important that he should not be disturbed when he is chewing on it. When you consider that he has had enough, discreetly remove it and dispose of it in the garbage bin. Do not give it to him out in the garden where he can bury it. He may then dig it up a few days later, by which time it will be riddled with maggots.

I have come across a number of cases where a child has happened to be standing over the place where a dog has buried a bone. Suddenly the dog attacks the child. The first hasty remark made by the owner or someone else usually is 'the dog attacked the child for no apparent reason'. But the real reason is hidden—hidden under the soil. The dog knows where his bone is, he can smell it, and he assumes the child is going to take it away, and therefore he protects it aggressively.

Remember to feed only raw bones to a dog and not cooked ones. When bones are cooked they become brittle and splinter into sharp pointed pieces. When swallowed these pieces can harm your dog's inside. Likewise never feed your dog any rabbit or poultry bones. These are needle-sharp and could also damage your dog internally.

In the last few years there has been a population explosion in the dog world. While there are fine pedigree dogs being bred by breeders who are experienced in their field, there are a great many dog owners who believe that their bitch must have at least one litter. These bitches may be cross-breds, non-pedigree, or pedigree stock, which have hereditary defects, bad faults in conformation, or undesirable temperament traits. Bitches and dogs in these categories should never be used for breeding. It is a fallacy to believe that every bitch must have a litter, and yet many owners go ahead with it and then have the bitch spayed afterwards. It makes no difference to her having puppies or not. Have the bitch spayed if you feel that life is going to be somewhat trying when she comes into season. Although bitches can be spayed before they have their first season, it is better for it to be done a few weeks afterwards. Having it done this way you are allowing her body to function at least once, even though it may inconvenience you for that period of about three weeks. And ensure that during this period she is not accidently mated.

Many local councils now charge a lower registration fee for spayed bitches as an incentive to dog owners to keep down the dog population. Some of these councils are also applying these lower registration fees to castrated male dogs. This is certainly a step in the right direction as it will help to reduce the vast number of unwanted puppies sired by roaming and uncontrolled male dogs. There are owners who have their dogs castrated for another reason, and that is to reduce the dog's aggression. In theory this result should follow, but in practice it depends upon the age of the dog when this operation is carried out.

If a dog is castrated at a very early age, say about seven to eight months, before he has started lifting his leg to urinate, he is likely to turn into a real old sook and he will never lift his leg, but squat. If he is done between nine and twelve months of age, during which time he is developing the art of lifting his leg, the results will be ideal; it can prevent aggression developing and it reduces the amount of distraction he will show towards other dogs. This is why male guide dogs for the blind are neutered at this age. The interesting thing is that for a short time after the operation, the dog will lift his leg, but then he will gradually adopt a squatting position when relieving himself. After this he will not lift his leg again. But if a dog is neutered, say at eighteen months of age or later, it is very unlikely that it will stop his aggression, if he has any. If aggression and strong distraction towards dogs have been allowed to develop up to that age, these traits will have become so firmly established in the dog that they will now be impossible to cure. Because his leg lifting has become such an instinctive habit, he will continue to lift it for the rest of his life. However, I am only generalising with these ages, and there are always exceptions to the general rule. I have known of a few cases where dogs have been neutered when they were a few years old and it has had the desired effect and reduced aggression, but there is certainly no guarantee that it will work; we just have to hope that it will.

5

Temperament

When you buy a dog you want to make sure he has a good temperament. While much of this can be inherited, much more will depend on how he is brought up. No matter what sort of breed he belongs to, or whether or not he is likely to be compatible to you, it is what you make of him that counts.

What makes up a dog's temperament? There are a number of traits which have been studied by trainers for years, and it is generally accepted that most, if not all, traits are partly mental and partly physical. It greatly depends on the way in which the dog is being handled or the environment he is in at the time. For example, a dog may be aggressive towards other dogs when he is with his owner, yet not aggressive when taken in hand by an experienced dog trainer whom he respects. Or a dog may work well at home, but not at a dog club, possibly because he is excited and distracted when he is in a large company of other dogs.

A partial list of temperament characteristics is as follows:

body sensitivity	capacity to learn
hearing sensitivity	willingness

nervousness	initiative
suspicion	attentiveness
sound shyness	concentration
anxiety	energy
animal aggression	curiosity
protective aggression	general distraction
pure aggression	animal distraction
apprehensive aggression	scent distraction
jealousy	excitability
wilfulness	dominance
stubbornness	submissiveness

Let us now take a closer look at each one.

Body Sensitivity
This is one of the most important characteristics to watch when you are training your dog on the leash. Some dogs are so highly sensitive that a little jerk on the leash will be all that is needed to get a good result, whereas a harsh jerk will make the dog afraid. Other dogs have a much lower body sensitivity. When a dog has an extremely low degree of this it will be almost impossible to train him. In most cases a low sensitivity is the result of the dog having received light niggling little jerks over a long period of time. The dog has therefore become so hardened to a physical jerk that

even when a much firmer jerk is given it has no effect.

Hearing Sensitivity

As with body sensitivity, this can range from high to low. Most dogs' hearing sensitivity lies somewhere between medium and high and this makes vocal control in training easy. One must be careful not to use too harsh a voice when correcting a highly sensitive dog, otherwise he could just go to pieces. Dogs which have very low hearing sensitivity and who give you the impression that they have not heard you, are also almost impossible to train. They usually become like this after continuous nagging and inconsistent training from their owners. Because they have been allowed to get away with everything they just turn on deafness to their owners' commands.

Nervousness

This is really a mental ailment and nothing can be done to cure it. It can be inherited, it can be the aftermath of distemper, and it can be the result of very bad treatment or of the dog having lived in a very restricted environment from puppyhood. I think the kindest thing to do in extreme cases of nervousness is to have the dog painlessly destroyed. On no account should he or she ever be used for breeding purposes.

Suspicion

This type of fear is natural in every dog and must not be confused with nervousness. Provided that the dog has been well conditioned during puppyhood, you should have no real problem with this. However, you must always be ready to accept that your dog may show this type of fear when he meets someone or something very unusual, and you must then coax him to overcome this suspicion.

Sound Shyness

This is also known as gun shyness. It is either an inherited trait or one that has been acquired because the dog has been subjected to frequent loud noises over a period of time. If the dog has more than a very small degree of it, it is virtually impossible to cure. If a dog has a small degree of it, there is always a slim chance of curing it by conditioning the dog to mild noises at first. This must be done very carefully and over a long period of time.

Anxiety

This is a type of fear where the dog becomes very concerned. The most obvious symptom is when the dog pants very rapidly. Anxiety often results when the dog has had an unpleasant experience, or has lived in a home where there was much human tension. When this tension goes, the dog often returns to normal.

Animal Aggression

Dogs can be fighters, chasers, or both. It is a bad trait and very hard to cure once it has become established. It can result from the fact that the dog was not socialised enough with other dogs during puppyhood, or was not corrected and handled properly by the owner when the aggression started. Dogs will fight over food, for social status, and because of sexual rivalry. These three situations will bring out this instinctive animal aggression as they always did when dogs lived in the wild state. An owner must take all necessary steps to prevent this trait developing.

Protective Aggression

Dogs can become protective of their owners, their home, the car, and many other things. Many owners, without realising it, allow their dogs to become too protective, and others even encourage it. Protection is all right up to a point and where it is warranted, but apart from this it can be very dangerous. It is often promoted when owners get too close to their dogs, even to the point of cuddling them as they sit or lie down with them on the grass. When the owners are in this position their dogs tend to protect them just as they would their own offspring.

It can start with the dog living in the bedroom with his master, who has been sick for some days. The dog will show this protective instinct towards other people coming into the bedroom, because by scent the dog will know that his master is ill. This is dealt with in more detail in the next chapter.

Pure Aggression

When a dog shows this type of aggression towards people he is actually using a means of defence. All dogs have a means of defence, ranging from attack to retreat. A dog who uses the attack method regards all people (except his master) as the enemy. The ideal dog is one who lies mid-way in this range, that is, one who will neither attack nor retreat but who is even tempered with everyone.

Apprehensive Aggression

Dogs who have this trait are commonly called 'fear biters'. They are either nervous or suspicious, and they also exhibit either protective or pure aggression. They are likely to bite, but only when frightened and cornered.

Jealousy

This is not a common trait, but it is one which you should watch carefully when handling more than one dog at the same time. It can soon lead to aggression. Often it is the result of the master fondling one dog more than the other.

Wilfulness

This is mainly inherent, and occurs more among male dogs than bitches. A wilful dog is one who is determined to have his own way, and a struggle can go on between you both. It is most important that you show him that there is going to be only one

boss—and that it is definitely going to be you!

Stubbornness

Unlike wilfulness, where the dog may want to do the exact opposite to what you want him to do, a stubborn dog will just sit there and refuse to do anything. Here again you have to exercise your authority by breaking that stubborn barrier down; make him do the exercise and do not forget to praise him even though you may not feel like it.

Capacity to learn

Usually if a dog has a good temperament, he will have a good capacity to learn. However, there are certain breeds which have a much greater capacity to learn than others, and even within each respective breed different strains and individual dogs will learn more and in a shorter time than others.

Willingness

Although most dogs like to please their owners, others lack the willingness. A good trainer can develop this and even raise it to a very high degree in a dog who had very little in the first place. In contrast a poor trainer can lower a dog's willingness even to the extent of destroying it altogether. So the development and degree of this characteristic depend mainly on the ability of the trainer.

Initiative

This is one of the traits which should be encouraged and yet controlled at the same time. Owners often complain that they have a very naughty dog. What they do not realise is that they have a very clever dog and that they should consider themselves fortunate that he excels in this way. He is a dog with tremendous brain power and he uses it for his own ends. What you have to do is to train him so well that he will use his initiative for you. Some of these so-called naughty dogs have been donated for use as guide dogs, and when trained have proved to be extremely good guides.

Attentiveness

Basically this is a natural characteristic and one which is present in all dogs to a greater or lesser extent. However, it needs to be developed and it is up to you as the trainer to use every means you can to develop your dog's attentiveness to you when training him.

Concentration

This is a characteristic which gradually develops after the dog has undergone training for a few weeks. Before he is trained he has nothing to concentrate on, so this cannot be assessed until he has some work to do. A dog with a good concentration is one who looks straight ahead and gets on with the job, so to speak. A dog with a poor concentration is one who looks aimlessly around as he walks along, giving you the impression that he is not really interested in anything. A good trainer can develop a dog's concentration to a certain extent, but much depends on whether or not the dog possesses this characteristic in potential form.

Energy

This refers to mental and physical activity. Some dogs are bubbling over with so much excess energy that they are uncontrollable. Such dogs need to be given training and work to do so that this energy is used up. When this is done the dog settles down, but regular work has to be kept up if everything is to be maintained on an even keel.

Curiosity

It is good when a dog shows a fair degree of this, for it will be a great help to you when you want him to investigate things in regard to which he has shown fear. Because he is curious his boldness will improve as you encourage him to approach these things.

General Distraction

Most young dogs are naturally distracted towards things, especially those that move. This distraction must be eradicated in training by the use of vocal and physical control, if you want a reliable working dog.

Animal Distraction

This generally applies to dog and cat distraction but it covers other animals as well. Strong distraction results when a dog has not been socialised enough with his own kind and other animals during puppyhood. It can be cured quite successfully during training, provided there is not a large degree of this trait.

Scent Distraction

This characteristic is the most natural one in a dog, because it is his number one sense. All scent distractions must be corrected in training. If they are not, he will show a partial or total disregard for you and be most unreliable. He will be using his nose for his own ends. Scent distraction must not be confused with nose work, which determines, for instance, whether or not he will be a suitable tracking dog.

It is interesting to note that although the hound breeds instinctively move with their noses glued to the ground, they can be taught to hold their heads up when they are trained in obedience.

Excitability

This is often seen in dogs who are high in energy and who are not taken out for walks, or whose owners are under extreme tension. Naturally all young dogs are excitable (there is usually something wrong if they are not), but this should be controlled by the owners. If a dog has a very excitable nature, see that he goes out for plenty of walks, and that you act calmly and talk firmly and quietly when controlling him. Quick movements on your part and your use of a sharp loud voice will excite him all the more and make him worse.

Dominance and Submissiveness

The domesticated dog of today still expresses his position on the ladder of social status, just as he did when he lived in the wild state. Dogs in a large pack range in order of social status from the most dominant, who is the pack leader, down to the most submissive. When you are caring for many dogs in kennels, it is vitally important that you pair off dogs who are completely different in their social positions. You will have no fear of a fight between a dominant dog and a submissive one. The former, being in charge, will not worry about the other challenging him, and the latter will be quite happy to accept the other dog as the boss. But if you kennel two dogs or two bitches of the same social status, then it is highly likely that disputes will arise between them. Such disputes often erupt into severe fights with possible fatal consequences.

You may now well ask, what is the ideal temperament? This really depends on what you want the dog for and what you want to do with him.

Dogs are needed for various kinds of work, such as police dog work, security work in the armed services, sheep herding, guiding the blind, show work, field trials, obedience trials, or they might just be wanted for family pets.

For each type of work there is a different combination of temperament characteristics which is considered ideal for the job. If a dog has the ideal temperament, for any work, then with expert training he can become a specialist within his own field.

However, as a general guide, you should have a dog who has no form of aggression or fear. His body sensitivity and hearing sensitivity should neither be too low nor too high. He should not be unduly distracted, but should be attentive, willing, and able to concentrate. It is also advantageous if he is curious, shows a fair degree of initiative, and has a great capacity to learn. It is a nuisance when such things as jealousy, wilfulness, stubbornness, and excitability exist in a dog, but these things can be overcome with training.

Although good dogs are bred, no one will ever be able to breed and train the perfect dog. You can only do your best. The responsibility is yours—it is what you make of it that counts.

6

The Dog's Senses

Dogs have senses just like we have, but they use them in a different way and in a different order of preference to the way in which we use ours.

Whereas man's number one sense is his eyesight, a dog's is his sense of smell. Because of this the work of man and dog complement that of each other as, for example, in crime detection work. A fingerprint expert, using his eyesight, can link the prints found at the scene of a crime with those of the person who made them, for no two people have the same fingerprints. A police dog, using his sense of smell, can find an article dropped or hidden by a person as he left the scene of a crime and can track where that person has gone, for no two people have the same scent. In both cases a wanted person is identified, but through the use of different faculties.

A dog's sense of hearing comes second to his sense of smell, while his sense of vision takes third place; then comes his senses of touch and taste. These are the five main senses but, like us, the dog has a sense of balance, a sense of heat, a sense of direction, and an incredible sense of time. In addition, there is evidence to suggest that he can sense the supernatural.

Now let us consider the dog's phenomenal sense of smell. Professor A. Stolk in his article 'Odour and Odour Diagnostics' says: 'If a dog's powers of smell are compared with those of the human being, our own performance pales into insignificance. As is well known, our own organ of smell, the olfactory mucosa, is particularly small. In addition, it is situated deep in the nasal cavity far from the zone of respiratory flow. To be able to smell something really well, we must therefore ensure that the air flow reaches the olfactory mucosa and its nerve cells by sniffing or snuffing. In man, the olfactory mucosa covers an area of no more than 5 square centimetres, which is particularly small when compared with the 150 square centimetres of the sheepdog. The olfactory cells have been counted in a number of breeds of dog and in man—the sheepdog has 230 million, the fox terrier 147 million, the dachshund 125 million and man 5 million. From this, it might be deduced that the sheepdog should be able to smell about 46 times better than man, but this is not the case. Using the olfactometer—a sensitive instrument for determining the powers of smell—it has been found that the sheepdog's powers of smell are, in fact, 1 million times better than man's. In assessing the power of smell, therefore, it is certainly not permissible to concentrate only on the surface of the olfactory mucosa or the number of olfactory cells it contains. Functionally speaking, special processes must take place in the dog which make its sharp sense of smell possible.'

The scent of a person is conveyed to a dog either by the wind or by the fact that the scent falls on to the ground and this provides a trail which the dog can track later. A dog will find a person very quickly when he is wind scenting, because the scent is active—it is being excreted by the person all the time. When a dog tracks a person who has laid a trail which is even a few minutes old, the scent is there but it is what I call a passive scent. In addition to this human scent the dog will also be tracking other smells produced by the person, such as those of crushed vegetation or insect life, and disturbed soil. A dog can detect differences of scent due to the sex and race of a person, as well as their occupation, and all of these scents will be found by the dog in a person's track.

A dog can also tell by means of scent what mood a person is in. Your dog will know if you are happy or miserable, relaxed or tense, angry or calm, frustrated or confident, tired, or even ill. You name it, he'll know it. One of the most common states that dogs can detect in their owners is the nervousness they show in a show or obedience trial ring. This unfortunately is transmitted to the dog and in consequence the dog plays up in some way or another.

It is interesting to note that the only time a dog cannot detect the scent of a human being is when the person is dead.

When the heart stops beating, the scent glands become inactive. Dogs have been known to find dead bodies in the Sinai Desert, but it is believed that they were attracted by the human scent which was still held in the clothing of the dead. Although it is generally recognised that human scent will evaporate in time, especially in conditions of extreme heat, sand covering a body will help to preserve the scent.

It has been known for a dog, particularly one who has lived very close to his master, to pine when the master has died. I suggest that he would sense that his master had gone, because the master ceased to throw off a scent any more. The dog would probably have acted in the same way had his master left him to go away for a holiday.

As mentioned in the last chapter, a dog will know when his master is ill by the scent that he excretes. On a recent occasion I had a terrible experience when I collapsed outside my bathroom with a severe internal pain. It was assumed later that it was caused by some obstruction. I lay there in agony for some minutes. Soon after this attack started, my Border Collie immediately lay down with her body around my head and remained with me until I recovered. She knew that there was something wrong. She never reacted like this at any other time.

That was a brief incident, but I would warn people who become sick not to have their dogs with them in their bedroom, as the dogs are likely to develop protective aggression. I remember a prime example of this with a guide dog and her blind master. He had been sick for a few weeks and his devoted guide dog stayed in his room all that time. After a week or two the dog showed protective aggression towards the visiting family doctor. This grew worse and the dog then showed aggression towards her master's wife. The case resulted in the dog having to be withdrawn from service and placed in another home as a pet. Later, the man recovered and was successfully trained with another guide dog. Had his first guide dog been kept in another room or outside during the illness, it is very unlikely that protective aggression would ever have developed in that bitch.

Towards the end of Chapter 3 I mentioned that when dogs meet they will sniff at particular parts of each other where scent glands are situated. I always find it interesting to see how dogs meet each other in the street. In the majority of cases they will sniff at each other's necks just below the ears, as well as under the chest, on the back near the base of the tail, halfway down the top side of the tail, and at the sexual organs.

Although I had often noticed this, it was not until the early 1960s that I became aware of the full significance of these areas on our dogs.

At that time I happened to be training a blind man from Israel with his second guide dog—a German Shepherd. One morning he informed me that he was certain that his dog was about to come into season. I told him that this was an impossibility as she had been spayed a few months earlier, and I was curious to know why he should think she was due. He told me that his first guide dog used to produce a musty smell on each side of her neck just below the ears about three weeks before she came into season (guide dogs were not spayed in those early days). He detected the same smell on his present dog and asked me to examine her. This I did. The dog's neck was perfectly clean, but I could smell this peculiar odour when I put my nose a centimetre or two from her neck.

On checking the dog's record card, we found that, had she not been spayed, on the basis of a six-monthly cycle she would be coming into season any day from then. Some months later I happened to pick up my own bitch in my arms and noticed she was producing the same smell. This only lasted for a few days, but within three weeks she too came into season. Our veterinary surgeon later explained that even when a bitch has been spayed there are other things in her body which will still be active, perhaps to a lesser extent, in her cycle of approximately six months.

A short time after this Professor T. J. Pickvance, M.A., B.Sc., of the Department of Extramural Studies, University of Birmingham, England, happened to be studying canine behaviour and aroused our interest in how dogs meet each other. One day he visited our Guide Dog Training Centre at Leamington Spa, and we carried out many experiments of introducing, from the large number of animals in the kennels, dogs and bitches which had never met each other before. About half were entire and the other half had been neutered. We observed that most of the dogs and bitches sniffed at each other's necks more than at the other areas of the body. You may care to see whether your own findings confirm this by observing the behaviour of strays as they meet each other on the streets.

A dog's hearing is highly sensitive. He has a far greater hearing range than we have. In training he learns to respond to different words. But really it is not so much the words we use as how we say them. If you say a word using a different intonation from normal he may not respond or he may show signs of being confused. On the other hand you can use some words, even the dog's name, with as many as three or four different tones to get the required results under various circumstances. For example, you could use the command 'Heel' in an inviting tone when you wish to walk forward at a normal pace, you could use it in a deeper tone when you want to move off at a slower pace, and in an excitable tone for a faster pace. On other occasions you may have to say 'Heel' in a very firm tone when your dog is distracted. So it is up to you to use your voice in the appropriate way to get the response you want.

Dogs have a keen sense of sight. A puppy which is only a few weeks old has a very short focal distance and as the weeks and months go by you will notice that his focal distance increases, more or less proportionately to his age. When he has become an adult he will be capable of focusing his eyes on something up to 1 kilometre away on the ground, and at greater distances when he spots an aeroplane in the air.

When I was an instructor at the Royal Air Force Police Dog Training Centre I had good opportunities to observe our German Shepherd dogs using their eyesight, as they were trained on Salisbury Plain, where one could see for great distances over open country. If a handler left his dog with someone, the dog would watch his handler walk further and further away. The further he went the stronger the dog's concentration became. Even at a distance of 1 kilometre the dog would not take his eyes off him. On the other hand, if the same dog was left with another person and hidden behind a vehicle while the handler walked away to the same distance and then the dog was brought out of hiding to face in the direction of his handler, the dog would not see him. But if the handler then waved his hand, the dog would suddenly be attracted by the movement and concentrate very strongly.

A dog sees life at a lower level than we do, and therefore the third dimension is more difficult for him to determine, but this can and does improve with experience. Let us consider the example of a dog who can jump across a 2-metre creek quite easily; we then ask him to jump over a 1½-metre broad jump consisting of several white boards, the tops of which are at slight angles (see Chapter 15). From our human eye level we can see what they look like and that they must be cleared in one leap, but from the dog's eye level it looks like a low, white platform. If you try and get him to clear that jump at the first attempt, he will more than likely take one leap on to the middle of it as if it were a low grooming table. In consequence he will knock the boards over and receive a nasty shock. So nasty in fact, that he will try to avoid the broad jump in future.

Dogs are very alert at night and will often show signs of suspicion. This is because street lights or other sources of illumination shining towards trees and other objects cast unusual shadows which make things look rather odd to dogs and they become very worried. But with dogs which are used to going out for walks in the dark, the chances of suspicion occurring in them will be much less.

Dogs are very competent at distinguishing silhouettes, as well as body and hand movements. Sheepdogs, in particular, watch and obey the movements of their owners. This sort of thing is an advantage when you want your dog to respond to a hand signal or facial expression, however, it can be a disadvantage when you use these signs quite unintentionally in the course of a conversation. Your dog may respond when you neither expect nor want him to do so.

The dog's sense of touch is variable, as mentioned in the previous chapter when I talked about body sensitivity. Some dogs are so highly sensitive that they are like fine bone china, while others at the other end of the scale are as tough as old boots. You should handle your dog according to his high or low degree of sensitivity.

Whenever you give physical praise to your dog you should stroke him on the head lightly and very slowly. This will get the best out of your dog; it will keep him calm, especially if he has an excitable nature, and you will also keep his attention on you and the work he is doing. Never, never pat your dog on the head or neck, or rough him up quickly, no matter how pleased you are with him. He is more than likely to move if you do this because you are disturbing him and exciting him. When I see people do this to their dogs I know they mean well, but how would they feel if someone patted them on the head and neck every few moments? They would soon get annoyed and probably end up with a headache.

As far as the dog's sense of taste is concerned, not a great deal is known except that, as in the human body, the sense of smell and the sense of taste are closely connected. Apart from this, there are some foods which some dogs prefer not to eat, and I think this is as much as we need to know.

Dogs have a sense of balance and it is important that you note this carefully, especially when training your dog to sit (explained in detail in Chapter 9). Much depends on how you use the leash when you want the dog to sit, stand, drop, etc. If the leash is used at the wrong angle, it can throw your dog off balance and he will either carry out the exercise incorrectly or not at all. I strongly advise people who train and show their dogs not to put the slip collar right up tight behind the dog's ears. I have seen dogs treated like this at shows and they have literally staggered about in the ring as if they were drunk.

I should like to see all dogs perform naturally on loose leads, and I should also like to see all judges penalise those handlers who have tight leads, as happens in obedience trials. It is good to see that some judges are already doing this. It would certainly stop a lot of handlers hiding certain faults, and dogs who show themselves by holding their heads up naturally to show alertness would be the ones which score.

I have many clients who come to me about problems they have with their show dogs. In the majority of cases I find they gait and stand their dogs on tight leads. As soon as I get them to work their dogs on loose leads they are quite surprised to see how much happier and relaxed their dogs are, and within a short time they are often on the road to success.

Like us, dogs have a sense of heat, and some breeds suffer more in high temperatures than others. By the same token some breeds, especially the short-coated ones, suffer from the cold. In a hot climate, you would be well advised to train your dog in the early morning or evening and not in the heat of the day. Also think of your dog's feet: avoid walking a dog on a tarmacadam surface which absorbs and holds the heat. If you put the back of your hand on a surface like this you will find out how painfully hot it is and you will better appreciate how it feels to your dog.

Now we come to the dog's sense of time. This is quite uncanny. A dog who works to a regular routine will soon get to know his on-duty and off-duty times. Even the untrained dog will get to know the regular family movements within his home and react accordingly at the right time. We are creatures of habit and tend to do certain things in a particular order at certain times of the day and week. Your dog will very soon learn what you are going to do next.

Very often he is stimulated by what he sees or hears you do. For example, if you take him out for a walk every evening at 8 p.m., and when you do he sees you put on your hat and coat or hears you take his leash out of a drawer, he will know by association of ideas that you are going to take him out for his regular walk. Let us suppose that one day you do not move out of your arm-chair to put on your hat and coat or get out the leash. By 8.05 p.m. he will draw your attention to the fact that you are overdue and will show you in his own doggy way that it is time for his walk. And he will not give you any peace until you take him out.

Blind people tend to do things to a more strict routine than others, and I have heard numerous reports from such people that their guide dogs know when they are going out, where they are going, how long they are going to stay, and so on. Many guide dogs know that there are seven days in a repeated cycle which we call a week, that each day is divided into periods which we call hours, and each hour is divided into periods which we call minutes. That is an extraordinary sense of time, you might say. Yes, it is, and you will learn how a dog can even judge time in seconds when you train your dog to stay (Chapter 10), and how you have to prevent him anticipating when the exercise is over.

Very occasionally I am asked if dogs have an extra sense by which they are able to detect the presence of supernatural beings—ghosts, evil spirits, or demons. For years I have been very curious about this, but the frustrating thing was that I could not find anyone who was an authority on the subject and who could explain it to me. Then one day in 1976 I met the Reverend Father Matthew G. F. Peiris, Ph.D., Diploma in Buddhist Studies, Vicar of the Church of St Paul the Apostle, Kynsey Road, Colombo 10, Sri Lanka, who is a world authority on demonology.

I asked Father Peiris if a dog can detect an evil spirit. He told me that during his ministry he had spoken to many mental-home patients who complained of one common factor—hearing a terrible, tormenting hoot. Since this hoot was not discernible by others, Father Peiris concluded that it was of a very high frequency, originating, not from a mental condition, but from a demonic source. He believed that under certain conditions dogs can hear this hoot. He also believed that in some cases dogs can see evil spirits—not necessarily with their eyes, but with a psychic sense, by which they become aware as if they were using their eyes.

Father Peiris' reason for coming to Australia was to visit a house in Sydney in which the owner's Dobermann dog would growl, bark, and attack an invisible figure in the house, regularly at midnight on Tuesdays and Thursdays. Some people thought that it was a chiming grandfather clock which stimulated the dog to react. They tried putting the clock forward, backwards, and even stopping it, but it made no difference. It was Father Peiris' contention that an evil spirit was visiting the house at this hour. He carried out a service of exorcism and the dog has been quiet ever since. Investigations made later revealed that a man had died in the house under circumstances sufficiently tragic to account for the appearance of his 'ghost'.

Father Peiris told me numerous accounts of how dogs in different countries have detected evil spirits, all of which would take too long to recount here. Some of the events were quite horrific, but after he had carried out services of exorcism the spirits were laid to rest and the dogs concerned showed no further reactions.

Mrs Irene Knight of the Elm Park Dog Training Club told me that a few years ago she and her family had a strange experience with their trained Golden Retriever, Robbie, while on holiday in Yorkshire. Early one morning she took him for a walk up a hill behind a farmhouse called Stainforth Hall. Although they had stayed at this camping site twice before this was a road they had not explored previously and at first Robbie set off at his usual full-steam-ahead pace. However, as they approached the hill he was very reluctant to accompany her and had to be coaxed and jollied along.

The next morning Jill, her daughter, decided to walk up this hill road with him, but came back after a very short time to say that Robbie had sat down at the bottom and refused to move. By now they thought something was a little queer about all this, so that evening Irene and her husband took him once again to the hill. Once again he sat down and they had to pull him along with them, he looking very sorry for himself; yet once they turned back he was very eager to get in front.

Some time later their son came across a book of Yorkshire ghost stories, one of which was about the ghost of a man and a dog who were seen walking up Dog Hill, on the same road behind Stainforth Hall. None of their family have previously believed in ghosts, in fact they still do not, but they cannot help wondering whether Robbie saw or sensed something which they did not.

What are the chances of your dog seeing an evil spirit? Who can say? It may be remote but the possibility is there. Nevertheless, it is fascinating to see how our dogs use all their senses and how they react instinctively. Dogs have very special purposes in the world and they well deserve their title of 'man's best friend'.

7

Basic Principles in Dog Training

THE BASIS OF GOOD DOG TRAINING

TEACHING
$\begin{cases} \text{Praise} \begin{cases} \text{Vocal} \\ \text{Physical} \end{cases} \\ \text{Correction} \begin{cases} \text{Vocal} \\ \text{Physical} \end{cases} \end{cases}$

RESULT:
$\begin{cases} \textit{The Dog gives:} \\ \text{Affection} \\ \text{Respect} \\ \text{Willingness to work} \end{cases}$

At school, when studying simple mechanics in elementary physics, I was taught the basic principle: Work put in equals work got out. It is a very short simple statement —easy to remember and useful to know. In later years I found that it truly applied to the training of dogs.

Fundamentally everything depends on you. The dog becomes what you make of him. When you train a dog you have to use two incentives: a positive one which is praise, and a negative one which is correction. Both have to be used in varying amounts depending on the dog, and both have to be applied vocally and physically. In return for all this work you put in you will get back true affection, respect, and willingness to work from your dog.

When you have to give a correction you must always follow it up by showing the dog what you want him to do, and then as soon as he responds, praise him. This is what I call a three-part correction. Let us imagine you are walking along with your dog at heel on the leash. He suddenly leaps at another dog. This is where you should instantly correct him by saying in a very firm tone 'No' and give him an appropriate jerk on the leash if it is necessary; immediately command him 'Heel' (for that is what you want him to do), and as soon as he responds praise him. The commands 'No', 'Heel', and 'Good Dog' can all be given in the space of two seconds. You may think that it is too difficult for a dog to comprehend such rapid vocal and physical control, but I can assure you he can do it, provided you time everything accurately and that you use the right tone of voice for each word. The word 'No' should be said very firmly and quickly, but not loudly. If you yell and scream in anger at your dog, it will probably make him worse, and you will upset yourself as well. The word 'Heel' should be given in a very meaningful tone, and 'Good Dog' in the most loving way you can to show how pleased you are with him.

Another principle closely linked with correction states that prevention is better than cure, or, to be more explicit, prevention should always be made before correction is necessary. Let us see how this applies in the situation where your dog leaps at another dog when he is supposed to be walking at heel. Firstly, it is up to you to be looking and thinking ahead as you approach another dog. You must also 'read' your own dog's mind and anticipate what he might do when he passes the other dog. Now rather than wait for your dog to leap at him, say in a slow warning tone, 'No; leave it; heel. No; leave it; heel.' Then, assuming he has behaved himself, as soon as he has passed the other dog, praise him by saying, 'Good dog; clever boy; very good.' So you see, you can use the word 'No' as a corrective word, or as a preventive measure. Your dog will understand you by the tone of voice you use.

And now we come to perhaps the most important principle in dog training. It is a principle which has seven parts and one which can be applied to everything you train your dog to do. These parts are as follows and must be used in this order:

1. Handler's decision
2. Capture the dog's attention
3. Handler's preparation
4. Handler's command
5. Handler's action
6. Dog's response
7. Praise

Let us imagine for example that you are going to train your dog to sit at a kerb. You make that decision a few metres before you get there. As you approach the kerb make sure you have his attention, and then prepare yourself by taking hold of the leash in the right hand and positioning your left hand above his hindquarters. Give the command 'Sit' and follow it up immediately with the physical action of holding the leash above his head and of pushing downwards and slightly forwards on his hindquarters with your left hand. The dog responds by going into the sit position. Upon that point of response you must praise him.

As time goes on, of course, all seven parts of this principle are not used. When you have fully trained your dog you may like to compete in an obedience trial. Your decision to sit the dog is replaced by a reflex action on your part to halt suddenly upon the order from the judge. The dog, having his attention on you, will sit automatically without any command or physical action. Praise is neither allowed nor is necessary until the entire exercise of heel work is over.

In all forms of training we have to start in a simple way, and in dog training we have to have a basis upon which we can build our exercises. This basis is known as the 'Straight Line Concept'. Ideally you should start teaching heel work to your dog in the longest straight line possible; then introduce turns with straight lines in between them. Later, the dog will be able to learn how to go around in circles, figure eights, and snake bends. One of the best examples of the use of the straight line concept is in the training of guide dogs for the blind. These dogs are trained to walk in a very long straight line, to keep in the centre of the pavement, to stop at all kerbs, and to cross straight over roads. When they have mastered all this they are trained to avoid all types of obstacles and after doing so to return immediately to the centre of the pavement. When crossing roads they are trained to stop for traffic and to proceed only in a straight line across the road when it is safe to do so.

Police dogs when being taught to track, start off by doing short straight tracks. Gradually deviations are made which the dogs cope with as they become more experienced.

When training your dog to do a particular exercise, or not to do something (like pulling the washing off the line or pulling up young trees in the garden), remember this principle: Always be in a position to do something about it. This not only means that you must be there with your dog, but it also refers to doing things in the correct way, such as placing your feet in the right position, jerking the leash at the right angle, using your hands in the right way, maintaining the right body posture, giving the right commands in the proper tone, and timing your actions correctly.

You will often hear an owner chastise his dog by the use of such words as 'You bad dog'. Frankly I do not believe that there are any bad dogs, but there are plenty of bad owners. If your dog does something which is wrong in your eyes, it is either because you have done something to him which you should not have, or you have not done something which you should have. Everyone is guilty of it at some time or other. So when your dog misbehaves, blame yourself. Then give just one word of reproof 'No', and proceed to train your dog properly. I shall always remember a motto we had at the Royal Air Force Police Dog Training Centre. Written in red on a large board in the main hangar where all personnel could see it daily were the words: 'Don't Punish Your Dog—Train it!'

A final principle which should be applied at the end of every training session you give your dog is to finish on a good note, and then give your dog the command to break off from work and go free. You could use a phrase like 'Go free' or 'Go on then', as long as it is a different command to any other he knows. He will soon understand that work is over, and that he can run off and play.

8

Training Equipment

In Chapter 3 I explained that all puppies should be fitted with small leather collars and become used to being lead on a leash. This is just a start, and as the puppy grows you will have to fit him with a larger collar and a stronger and heavier type of leash. It is possible to train some dogs—those with a high body sensitivity—on a fixed leather collar, but the vast majority need to have a slip collar of some description.

The most popular one is the slip chain collar. This is available in various lengths and with different sizes of links. It should never be too long, but you should just be able to put it on and take it off your dog's head comfortably. If it is too long, it will probably come off when he is running, or he may put his foreleg through it as he jumps over a high obstacle, or if he is a small dog it may hang down and get in the way of his feet as he comes towards you. You will also find it hard on your hands if you have to take hold of it when you are teaching him basic training, which I shall come to later.

With small- to medium-size dogs the fine-link slip-chain collars are good. With larger dogs, collars having larger and longer links

are better; they have a better training effect on larger dogs, and for this reason are used extensively throughout the world in the training of police dogs and guide dogs for the blind. Also they do not cut the dog's coat around the necks as much as the finer link ones do.

There is a right way and a wrong way of putting a slip collar on a dog's neck. The right way is shown in fig. 20. The links run from the clip of the leash through the large round ring and *over* the top of the dog's neck and around to the round ring. As the dog is on your left side, when you give him a jerk and relax the leash the collar will instantly tighten and then automatically unfold itself.

The incorrect way is shown in fig. 21 where the links run from the clip of the leash through the round ring and *under* the dog's neck and around to the round ring. If you give a jerk on the leash and relax it, the collar will instantly tighten but will not automatically unfold itself.

The only exception to this rule of putting a slip-chain collar on a dog, is when the dog is going to be trained on the handler's right side. This sometimes occurs

Above: Fig. 20. The correct way of putting on a slip-chain collar. The fine links come from the ring attached to the leash, through the other ring, and continue *over* the top of the dog's neck. *Below left:* Fig. 21. The incorrect way of putting on a slip collar. The fine links are going through the ring and underneath the dog's neck. When the leash is relaxed the collar will not loosen as it should. *Below right:* Fig. 22. The leather slip collar is ideal for dogs who are very sensitive

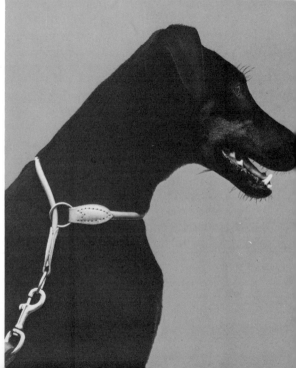

when the owner is disabled in the use of the left hand or arm, or has had the left arm amputated. An important point to remember for anyone who has to train his or her dog on the right is that instructions in training (e.g., left, right, left-about, right-about turns) have to be given in reverse. This is covered in Chapter 9.

Although most dogs need to be trained on chain-type slip collars, there are others for whom the chain is too severe. Its use will effect their body sensitivity and have the effect of making them cringe and lose willingness. A slip collar made of leather, cord, or a broad strip of nylon is much better for these types of dogs (fig. 22). It will still do the job you want it to do, without being severe in any way.

The double-action slip collar has its merits (fig. 23). When you give a jerk on the leash, the collar tightens, but only a little. This also is ideal for a sensitive type of dog. However, it has one disadvantage and this is that it can only be used for one size of dog. You cannot use it on a range of dogs with varying sizes of heads and necks, as you can with an ordinary slip collar.

The quality of collars manufactured to-day varies considerably. When you purchase one I advise you to check it very carefully. Examine the welding in the links, and compare the stitching with that of other collars. Run the collar through your fingers very slowly and make sure that everything is smooth. Look for sharp pieces sticking out, no matter how small. They may dig

Fig. 23. The double-action slip-chain collar is also ideal for sensitive dogs. When a corrective jerk is given, the collar will tighten so far but no further

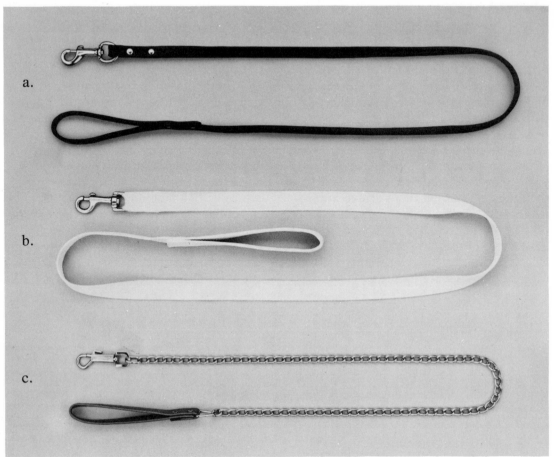

Fig. 24. *Leashes* (a) 120-cm leather training leash; (b) 150-cm webbing leash. Ideal for suspicious dogs who sometimes need to have a large area of independence; (c) chain leashes are not suitable for training, but are useful in tethering dogs for short periods of time

into the dog when you jerk the leash, and you may cut your fingers on them if you take hold of the collar quickly when training your dog.

The best type of leash is a leather one fitted with a solid snap hook (fig. 24). Ideally, this should be secured with two rivets or be hand stitched. The same should apply to the handle at the other end of the leash. Before leather leashes are used it is best to soak them in neat's-foot oil or treat them with saddle soap. This will prevent cracking, preserve the leather, and make the leash supple and comfortable to handle.

Leashes made out of webbing material are very good. They are strong and comfortable to handle, and you get a firm grip on them. Nylon leashes, although they are strong, are rather slippery and therefore hard to grip. The chain leash is about the last thing you want to get for training. If

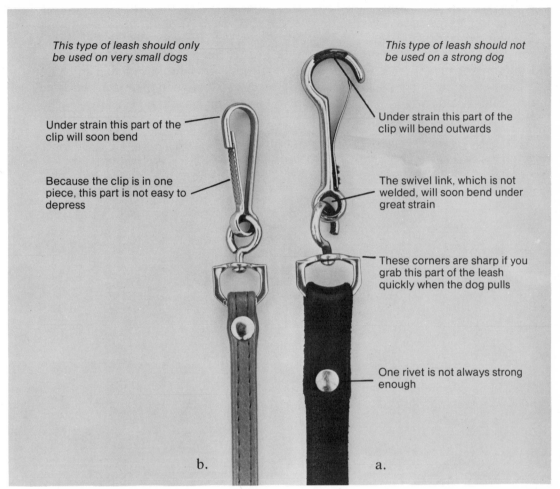

This type of leash should only
be used on very small dogs

This type of leash should not
be used on a strong dog

Under strain this part of the
clip will soon bend

Under strain this part of the
clip will bend outwards

Because the clip is in one
piece, this part is not easy to
depress

The swivel link, which is not
welded, will soon bend under
great strain

These corners are sharp if you
grab this part of the leash
quickly when the dog pulls

One rivet is not always strong
enough

b.

a.

Fig. 25. Two Types of Leash Clips

you use one of them, your hands will really suffer! People buy them because they have a dog who chews through leather leashes. A dog who does this should be corrected immediately in training. When you are not training your dog do not leave the leash lying around for him to chew, but put it away in a drawer or somewhere where he cannot get at it.

The only time I would use a chain leash is when I found it necessary to tie up the dog for a short time; a potential chewer would probably bite through a leather leash in a few seconds and be off.

It is very important when buying a leash to ensure that the clip is strong enough for the dog it is going to hold. The clip shown in fig. 25a is all right for small dogs which are not very strong. When it is used on a strong dog the hook gradually bends outwards and the spring is rendered useless. The swivel link, not being welded, also pulls out and the next thing you know is that your dog has got away.

A smaller clip shown in fig. 25b can be rather difficult to operate between finger and thumb, because it is all in one piece. The clip will soon bend out, even under a moderate strain, when you give your dog jerks on the leash to correct him.

So when you purchase equipment for your dog be very choosey. Select good-quality leashes and collars which are comfortable to handle, reliable in taking the strain, effective in their use, and which will last for many years (fig. 26).

Fig. 26. *Training Collars*   (a) Buckled leather collar; (b) Fine link slip-chain collar; (c) Large link slip-chain collar; (d) Rolled leather slip collar; (e) Flat leather slip collar; (f) Nylon webbing slip collar; (g) Double action slip-chain collar with double chain neckpiece

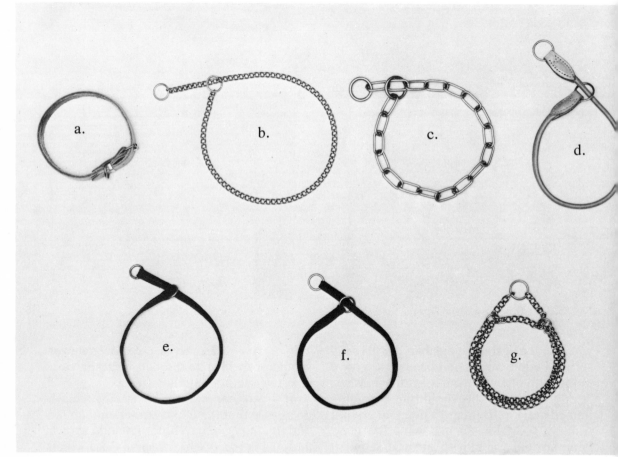

9

Heel Work

The first exercise you must train your dog to do whether he is an adult or a puppy aged four months or more is to walk at heel. Most people do not realise the importance and necessity of training their dogs before they have become fully grown and are too strong to hold. By this time they have been allowed to have too much of their own way and show little or no respect for their owners. Heel work gets the dog's respect quicker than any other exercise.

Nearly every untrained dog will pull on the leash, and the main reason for this is that the owner holds on too tightly to it. Imagine that you had a horse and cart, and one day you put into the cart a heavier load than the horse was used to pulling. What would his reaction be in moving it forward? He would pull harder, would he not? Now when you hold on tightly to a dog on a leash you are very much like the cart in that you are putting an extra load on to the dog; so what will he do? Like the horse he will pull harder. For this reason you should not hold on tight. But that is only half the problem. A dog will still pull for other reasons, such as being distracted towards other animals, being eager to get

out for a walk, trying to catch up with another member of the family who is walking ahead, or wanting to get home for his feed. In all these cases and any others the dog must be corrected and trained to walk at heel with his head beside you.

The procedure is as follows: Firstly, get your dog to stand or sit beside you on the leash. Hold the handle of the leash in your right hand and also grip it at another point a little further down using the thumb and first finger of your right hand. Have your right hand in a relaxed position to the centre of your body (fig. 27). You will now see that the rest of the leash (between your right hand and the dog's collar) will hang in a U shape. Do not hold on to the leash with your left hand. This is to be used only for giving corrective jerks.

Forward
Having decided what you are going to do, made the necessary preparations, and captured your dog's attention, you are now all set to carry out the remaining four parts of the seven-point principle. In an inviting tone, give the command 'Rex, heel'. Then comes your action where you just step forward. This is followed (hopefully) with

Fig. 27. 'Rex, heel.' Always make sure you have your dog's attention when you are about to go forward

the dog responding by moving his first paw forward (fig. 28) and on this point of response you must praise him immediately, 'Good dog. Very good'.

Pulling

Assuming that he continues to walk at heel, keep telling him what a good dog he is. Then comes the time sooner or later (in fact it is nearly always within the first few metres) when he will start to pull. When this happens grip the last piece of the leather leash (which joins the clip) in your left hand, say in a firm voice 'Heel', and jerk him straight back at his shoulder height; then immediately let go and stand still (fig. 29). Wait for a few seconds and, provided he has not moved, invite him again 'Rex, heel', step forward, and praise him as he responds. Most dogs pick up this exercise very quickly, but I have had some dogs brought to me who were very headstrong because they had been allowed to get away with pulling on their leashes for a very long time. It was not uncommon for me to have to correct such a dog about twenty times in the first thirty metres, and because of this consistent training the dog suddenly realised that it was no good trying to have his own way any longer and that he just had to walk at heel where he was going to be praised.

There are two very important points which I must emphasise in this correction. The first is that when you jerk back make sure that you jerk back horizontally at the dog's shoulder height. If you jerk backwards and upwards you will be wasting much of your energy in trying to lift the dog off the ground. Not only will this wear you out, but the dog will not learn as well. As soon as you have jerked, let go. If you hold on for even an extra second, the dog will feel a load on the other end of the leash and will strain against it. The second

Left: Fig. 28. The correct position of the dog when walking at heel. *Right:* Fig. 29. A pulling dog must be corrected immediately. Take hold of the leash near the clip, command 'Heel', and jerk straight back along the dog's back; let go and stand still

point is that it is vitally important that you stop still. In refusing to go any further you are showing the dog that you are the master and that he must walk beside you and no further in front. When you have stopped, if he moves forward again, stand your ground, command 'Heel', jerk back, and let go. He may try this a few times, but show him that you are going to stay there and that you are going to correct him consistently.

This act of standing still is the main secret in heel work. Over the years I have had clients who declare that they have been attending obedience dog training clubs for as long as two years and yet their dogs still pull. Seeing them work for just one minute is enough to show why the dog still pulls. The owner jerks back consistently, although not always horizontally, but does

not stand still. The dog thinks, 'Well, if I pull, I'll get these jerks, but we will still keep on the move.' It does not take long to correct this fault when the owner is shown how to deal with it by stopping.

I suggest that dog club instructors look very closely at this problem. It cannot be corrected in a class where handlers and their dogs walk in line directly behind those in front of them, but it can be corrected if the participants walk in a line abreast of each other. The main thing is that every handler should be shown this technique, which can then be practised at home.

Distractions

This technique can also be used when your dog is distracted towards something over on your right. A dog can push across in front of your legs only if he is allowed to be too far forward. Always stop and get him right back so that his head is beside your leg. It does not matter if he stands or sits, as long as his head is beside you.

If your dog is distracted to the left, then jerk him horizontally to the right (across in front of your left knee) at his shoulder height, but keep going; do not stop. If he is distracted to the rear, then jerk forward at this height and keep moving. If you as much as hesitate, let alone stop, your dog will have won by being distracted towards something else while showing a total disregard for you. If he is distracted towards a ground scent beneath him, then jerk vertically upwards.

With all these distractions, no matter in which direction they are, give the word of reproof 'No', followed immediately by 'Heel', then praise as the dog responds. But if the dog wanders away from the heel position because of lack of concentration, then say 'Heel' and encourage him into you. You will have to use your judgement as to whether he is distracted or just lacks concentration. If it is the latter, there is no need to say 'No'.

Sit

As you walk with your dog you decide to make him sit. Ensuring that you have his attention, prepare by putting the clip-end of the leash into your right hand (you will now have three parts of the leash in your right hand). Give him the quick, sharp, but quiet, command 'Sit', pull the leash up vertically above his head, and simultaneously push his hindquarters down and slightly forwards with your left hand, thus ensuring that his hind feet go towards his fore feet (fig. 30). Upon his response immediately slacken the leash by releasing that third point on it so that it is comfortable around his neck. At the same time bring your left hand round to praise him

on his head. This should be done in very slow soothing strokes which will keep him calm, especially if he is a young excitable dog, and help to keep his attention on you and the work he is doing. As I have said before, do not pat or stroke your dog up vigorously, no matter how pleased you are with him. This can have a disturbing effect on him and is likely to cause him to move.

When sitting your dog, watch your right hand all the time and make sure that you pull the leash up vertically. If you pull backwards and upwards at the same time that you push downwards and forwards your dog will feel as if he is going to be turned over on his back and will naturally resist sitting. This is where his sense of balance is shown. It is a bad thing to look at your left hand during this exercise, because if you do you will not see what your right hand is doing. So feel with your left hand and place it on the dog's hindquarters with your thumb facing away from you, just as you would if you threw a cricket ball underarm. This way you will have the best control, using all your fingers, the thumb, and the palm of your hand as in figs 30 and 31. If you use your hand the other way (with your thumb turned towards you) you can only use your thumb and first finger, and you are likely to dig these into his kidney region which will be very unpleasant for him (fig. 32).

Apart from using both hands in this exercise, discipline yourself to keep your feet facing straight in the direction you are going. Many people turn their feet towards their dogs and even step towards them. Consequently the dog moves away and sits crookedly. So face straight ahead and teach the dog to sit close beside you and parallel with your feet. Also bend at the knees and keep the weight of your body over your feet. This will make the whole action much

Above: Fig. 30. The correct way of sitting a dog. The leash is held firmly above the dog's head and the hindquarters are pushed down and forwards with the left hand. *Below:* Fig. 31. With the thumb facing to the left you will have the best control. Remember to keep your feet pointing in the direction you are going

Above: Fig. 32. The incorrect way of sitting a dog. If the leash is pulled back as the left hand pushes down, the dog is likely to resist or sit in a bad position. You should not turn into the dog as he will learn to sit at an angle towards you. The left hand should be turned the other way as in figs 30 and 31

easier for you to carry out. Those who lean over their dogs too much pull backwards on the leash and get resistance from the dog, as explained earlier.

One of the best places to practise heel work is on a footpath. Keep in the centre and the kerb and fence will provide good guide lines for you to keep straight (fig. 33).

Right-About Turn

This is the only turn involved during your dog's first few lessons of heel work, in

Above: Fig. 33. One of the best places to teach a dog heel work is on a long straight footpath. *Right:* Fig. 34. *The Right-About Turn* Whatever the dog's height it is very important to keep your hands at that height when doing this turn

which you are also laying the foundation of the straight line concept in his mind. Until now you have held the leash in your right hand. For convenience, when you carry out this right-about turn, take the entire leash in your left hand in one grasp so that you take hold of it about 25 cm away from the clip. This will leave your right hand free so that you can pat your right leg, to encourage your dog to do a

right-about turn as you say 'Rex, heel'. While you do this keep your left hand down to his height (fig. 34), for it might be necessary to give him a jerk if, and only if, he does not respond to your encouraging command. As soon as you see him give the first sign of response to the turn, praise him. In doing this manoeuvre make sure that you turn on the spot and return along the same line that you came on. If you do a

U turn, your dog will bow out. Ensure at all times that the leash is slack, even when there is only the 25-cm length between you and the dog. If you pull it tight, he will pull outwards.

Right Turn

Once the dog has learned the right-about turn, the right turn is very easy. Exactly the same command and action are made (fig. 35), the only difference being that this is a 90-degree turn, whereas the other is 180 degrees. Now regardless of whether you intend competing in obedience trials or not, if you want to capture the best attention from your dog, give the command first, turn your feet on the spot as he responds, and then walk off in the new direction, praising him. You will get much more out of him this way than if you gradually went round to the right, which would be more of a right wheel than a sharp right turn. As soon as you have done a right, or right-about turn you can transfer the leash back into your right hand.

Left Turn

I always think that this is the easiest turn of the lot. With this turn there is no need to transfer the leash from one hand to the other. All you have to do is to take hold of the leash near the clip with the finger and thumb of your left hand, give the command 'Heel', jerk the leash straight backwards in perfect line with the dog's spine, simultaneously pivot on the ball of your left foot towards the left, and bring your right foot around and continue walking in the new direction (fig. 36). You should let go of the leash immediately you have given the backward jerk. The jerk after all is to stop the dog advancing any further and in that fraction of a second you step around in front of him. Make sure that you do not stop but

Left: Fig. 35. *The Right Turn*   To capture the full attention of the dog, make right turns sharp and attract the dog by patting your leg as you use his name and say 'Heel'. *Right:* Fig. 36. *The Left Turn*   Give him the command 'Heel', jerk straight back along his back, pivot on the left foot, and step around sharply with the right foot

keep on the move as you step around with your right foot, which is the outside foot as far as your dog is concerned. Later when he sees your body turn and your right foot come around, he will turn his head in the same direction and his body will follow. If you unintentionally step across with your left leg first, you are likely to tread on his paws. You can leave the dog's name out of this turn as you have to go around the dog. You want to retain the use of his name for the right and right-about turns where the dog is on the outside and you have to call him in to you as you turn.

Left turns can be very useful in training an over-exuberant dog. If you go around long enough in a small square (about 6 metres square) doing left turns, you will find that he will soon keep back to heel because you keep chopping off his advance.

With a lagging dog you need to adopt the opposite method, whereby you go around in a very large square doing right turns, walking at a fairly brisk pace. The dog, being on the outside, has a longer distance to cover and will have to hurry in order to keep up with you. Unless the dog is stubborn, do not jerk him forward. This will destroy what willingness he has. Instead give him a lot of encouragement and pat the front or inside of your left leg with your left hand. Never pat the left side of your leg as this will make him either drop back further, or walk wide for fear of having his nose knocked by your flapping left hand. If you stop and think about what he has to put up with, you will soon realise why he reacts in this way.

Crooked Sits

Most dogs sit crookedly, too far forward, or in a floppy way, and unless these faults are corrected they become bad habits in dog training. There are several ways of correcting these faults. Obviously the first way is to make sure he sits properly in the first place, or to prevent him doing the wrong thing with the use of your hands. Some people step forward and have another go at sitting the dog straight, others bring the dog all the way around them to heel and try again, while others do all the work and just heave the dog into position and the dog just lets them do it.

The most successful method, which I believe is the best, was taught to me years ago by Sanden Moss, a very experienced brilliant trainer in England. (See fig. 37.)

Let us suppose then that your dog has sat crookedly and too far ahead as well. Place your left hand on the leash near the clip with your thumb on the top. Keeping your right foot where it is and facing in the direction you have been going, cast your left foot back in a slight arc behind your right foot. As you do this, command the dog in an inviting tone 'Rex, heel', and entice him to follow your left hand (which holds the leash) and turn in towards you, then slightly away as he comes back and then in towards you again. As he does the last turn, bring your left foot forward to your right foot. Rex, thinking you are going forward, will come in beside you, whereupon you make him sit. The pattern that you have shown him is like a letter S only in reverse. Like all other aspects in heel work ensure that your left hand holds the leash at the dog's height until you make him sit, when it must be held vertically above his head in the right hand as you push downwards and forwards with your left. When you carry out a correction like this leave nothing to chance—use your hands to set him up in the right position. During this correction praise him as he responds so that he will associate the correction with pleasure.

69

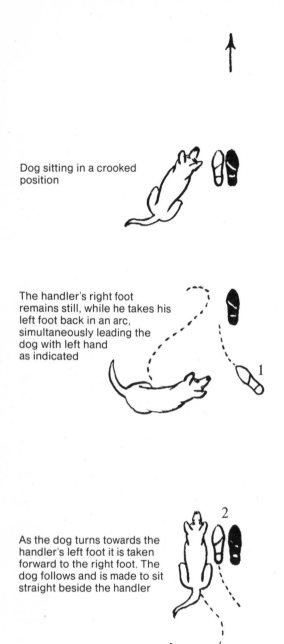

Dog sitting in a crooked position

The handler's right foot remains still, while he takes his left foot back in an arc, simultaneously leading the dog with left hand as indicated

As the dog turns towards the handler's left foot it is taken forward to the right foot. The dog follows and is made to sit straight beside the handler

Fig. 37. The Crooked Sit Correction

Wide Sits

The dog who sits wide usually heels wide. The main reason for this fault is because the owner is inclined to walk into his dog and, if he does not walk into him, he steps into him when coming to a halt. This not only affects the sit, but the stand and down positions as well. In correcting this fault two things have to be done. Firstly, the handler must concentrate on walking straight and not into the dog at any time. Secondly, a correction like that used for a crooked sit can be made with an additional side-step in it.

This correction is the same up to the point where you turn the dog in towards you (just when you are about to take your left foot forward), but before you move your left foot forward take a pace directly to the right with your right foot, then take your left foot forward and against your right foot (fig. 38).

You will now notice that both you and your dog have shifted over sideways to the right of your original position. You have in fact drawn your dog closer to you. When you do this correction you can say 'Heel close', and this extra word 'close' will prove to be of great value in the future. Not only will your dog learn the meaning of the word, but he will learn to do a short cut by shuffling in sideways to you instead of going through the whole procedure I have just explained, and of course this is the end result you want.

When a dog has a habit of walking wide this method can be applied when going forward, while heeling, and when coming to a halt. You need to have an open piece of ground for this as you will be walking in progressive parallel lines to your right.

With much practice a dog can be made so conscious of the words 'Heel' and 'Heel close' that you can get him to heel sideways, crossing his legs as he does so (like a horse does in a dressage event).

After this you can train your dog to heel backwards a few metres to the command 'Heel back'. You would never be required to do these moves in obedience trials, but from a daily practical point of view they can be very useful.

Left-About Turn

There are two recognised ways of doing this turn. One way is known as the pivot turn, in which you do a left-about turn but the dog does a right-about turn. All you have to do is to transfer the leash from one hand to the other and back again as you turn. While most people favour this turn because it is easy, I do not. In my opinion you have not taught your dog anything new because he has already learned how to do a right-about turn. I therefore favour the method where both handler and dog turn left-about. Most people find this way very hard, for they either crash into their dogs or, if they take special care, they will only be able to get round in front of their dogs by going around in a gradual U shape. Either way would be penalised in obedience trials.

As you walk with your dog at heel, place your left hand (with thumb on the top) on the leash next to the clip. Say 'Heel' in a slightly drawn out but inviting tone, and quickly step around in front of your dog so that you are both face to face. Then apply the correction of a crooked sit exercise, i.e., you guide him to come into your side by taking your foot backwards and then forwards. As soon as he is beside you walk forward and this will take you back along your original path (fig. 39).

It does not take long for your dog to learn that he has to revolve with you and he will soon know which turn you are going to make by the intonation of your com-

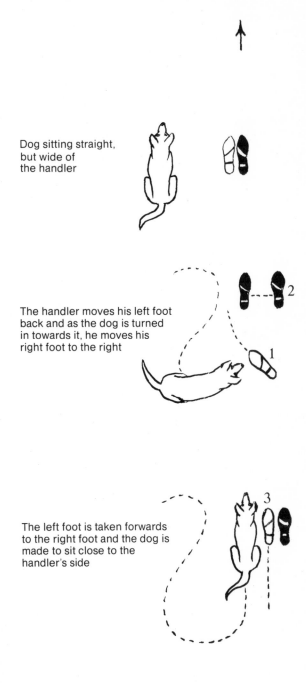

Dog sitting straight, but wide of the handler

The handler moves his left foot back and as the dog is turned in towards it, he moves his right foot to the right

The left foot is taken forwards to the right foot and the dog is made to sit close to the handler's side

Fig. 38. The Wide Sit Correction

71

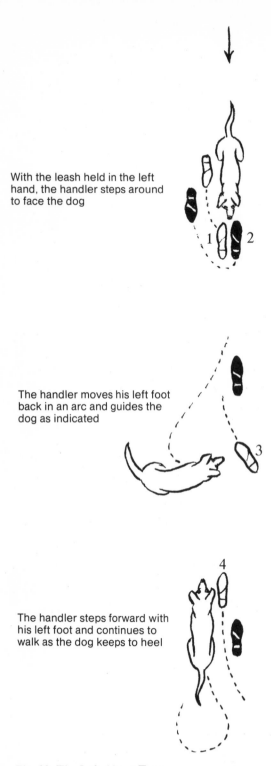

With the leash held in the left hand, the handler steps around to face the dog

The handler moves his left foot back in an arc and guides the dog as indicated

The handler steps forward with his left foot and continues to walk as the dog keeps to heel

Fig. 39. The Left-About Turn

mand. Later he will recognise that it is a left-about turn by the way you turn your entire body around 180 degrees to the left. Later on you will not even have to give him the clue with your voice or use your left hand and foot to guide him. He will just revolve with you as he sees you turn in this direction. This turn is very easy to do when you know how, but do not attempt to do it until you have mastered all the other basic moves in heel work.

Figure Eight

This is one of the last things you should teach your dog in heel work. If it is introduced too early, many dogs get bored with it and they lag and lose willingness and concentration, which is a great pity. Make sure that your dog knows how to heel really well before you teach him this exercise.

In obedience trials you are required to heel your dog in the figure eight twice around two stewards standing 3 metres apart. There will also be at least one halt during this exercise, which is often given when your dog is very close to one of these stewards. The reason for this is to see if the dog will sniff at that person, in which case points will be lost for scent distraction.

This figure eight is very short in distance and the clockwise and anti-clockwise loop turns around the two stewards are rather tight. This often makes a dog slow up, especially if you go around too slowly. Therefore in your daily training I suggest you start by going around two poles in a much larger circuit. Each loop turn could have about a 2-metre radius and the poles could be about 6 metres apart. This will enable you to keep your speed up and, as the days go by, you can gradually diminish the size of the figure eight. It is the only portion of heel work which is in a definite pattern, and dogs soon come to realise this.

Because of this, some dogs lose concentration and lag. One thing you can do to overcome this fault, if it occurs, is occasionally to continue to make a complete circuit around the pole which you encircle in a clockwise direction. Go around twice if you like, which will really make your dog hurry and concentrate to keep up with you. But a word of warning here, don't do it more than twice, otherwise you may get giddy and perhaps fall over. Never mind, training is still great fun!

10

Sit-Stay

The sit-stay exercise is the vital stepping-stone between basic heel work and the recall on the leash. It should be taught after the first few days of heel work which have included the forward, the sit, the three turns, and the correction of the crooked sit.

Having given your dog some heel work for a few minutes, which will help him to settle down, especially if he is excited, sit him at a particular spot. Behind a crack on the pavement, beside a particular weed on the grass, or by any other small landmark will do. You must always make a mental note of the exact position where you have made him sit and the direction he is facing. If, when you are teaching him to stay, he moves from that spot for some reason or other, it is imperative that you take him back to it and the same direction and then start the exercise all over again. If you were to re-sit him on a different spot, say 50 centimetres in front of his original stay position, he would have won half a metre and he will probably try it again and again. He will know the original spot that you take him back to because of his own scent upon it.

As soon as you have made him sit hold the leash entirely in your left hand (approximately half a metre away from the clip) and vertically above his head. It must not be tight, but just slack. Keep your body upright and give *one* command 'Stay' without his name. At the same time you can give a hand signal with your right hand by swinging it up from your right side, slightly in front of him, and up to your face. This will help to capture his attention as your eyes take over. It is amazing how you can control your dog with your eyes, and as you do, step around in front of him and face him all the time (fig. 40). Your left hand, which is holding the leash, must maintain its position directly over his head. If he attempts to move, your hand is in the best position to correct him by giving him a quick upward jerk, to be relaxed immediately as you say 'No'. Here is a perfect example of the training principle mentioned in Chapter 7, namely, always be in a position to do something about it. After a few seconds, slowly return to his side by the way you left him. Wait for a few seconds and then slowly and gently praise him.

Now let us look at those points in more

Right: Fig. 40. *The Sit-Stay* In this first stage keep the leash just slack but vertically above the dog's head so that you can correct him with an upward jerk if he moves

74

detail. You give him only one command 'Stay'. I always believe in looking ahead to the future and one day you will want to leave him in the stay position while you go completely out of sight. You will not be able to keep saying 'Stay. Stay. Stay'. So your dog might as well get used to having only one command now and for ever more. Because you have used his name with going forward in heel work, he may confuse these two exercises and move. So it is best with all stationary exercises (the sit, stay, stand, and down) to exclude his name, but do use his name if you want to when training him in exercises of movement as in heel work and the recall. Keep upright when you give the command 'Stay' so that he looks up to you as the master. There is no need to bend down to his ear, like some people do, and yell '*Stay*'. He is not deaf!

In the early lessons of the stay show him that it is a completely different exercise to the heel, by stepping right round in front of him to face him, and not stepping straight forward and then turning about to face him. He may mistake this latter movement as a going forward to heel.

From the time you say 'Stay' to the time you praise him at the end of the exercise, have the word 'No' on the tip of your tongue. You will not always know when he is going to move but, if you can get that word out quickly with a quick upward jerk on the leash, you will at least arrest him on the spot. However, you can often read your dog well enough, and anticipate his intentions of moving. When you see these signs, give him the word 'No' in a slow warning tone, as much as to say 'Don't you dare think about it. I'm watching you. I'm the master!'

Do not leave your dog in the stay position for long. About ten seconds is enough to start with and, as you return, walk back slowly to his right side. If you are too quick, you may disturb him and he will move.

Whenever you return always stand quite still beside him before you give him praise. It is very bad when people praise their dogs as soon as they get back to them. Within a very short time their dogs anticipate this and start getting up before their owners have returned to them. So keep your dog guessing as to when the exercise has completely finished. Dogs have an incredible sense of time. Let us imagine that on every occasion when you return to your dog you praise him after a time lapse of four seconds. One day you decide to wait much longer, but by the time five or six seconds has elapsed your dog will probably have pushed his nose into your hand to draw your attention to the fact that you are one or two seconds overdue in giving him the customary praise. One could be excused for thinking that dogs had stop-watches built into their brains! Anyway this is how clever and accurate they can be. So, rather than fall into this habit of having a set time to conclude the exercise, vary the time that elapses from when you return to him to when you praise him. It may be four seconds, then nine, three, ten, seven, five or six seconds. As long as you vary the time you will keep him guessing.

As soon as you have done this stay and it is successful do another one. This time, when you have stood out in front of him, try moving to his left and then around to his right in a semi-circular fashion. Ensure that you keep your left hand above his head the whole time. This means of course that you cannot move any further from him than your arm's length. Then return to his side. Wait a few seconds; then praise and take him forward at heel.

Always accept the possibility that most

Fig. 41. As the dog grasps the exercise you can go a little further away

dogs will move during these initial stages of the stay exercise. It is not that they are disobedient, they just do not understand yet. What you have to do is to make it as easy as possible for your dog to understand.

If he does move off the original spot say 'No'; then 'Rex, heel' as you immediately return on to your original spot (from where you said 'Stay') and bring him into the heel position by using the correction of the crooked sit. This is the quickest method, and you cannot afford to waste valuable time. All corrections in dog training must be made in the minimum amount of time.

Two common errors handlers make which cause their dogs to move are: praising their dogs when they are standing out in front of them, and bending down even slightly when saying 'No'. In both cases dogs are likely to move. In the first case the dog likes praise and naturally wants to get to his master, and in the second case he has always noticed that his master has bent down to him when calling him. It is only natural then that he will try to come to his master. So remember with the stay all praise is left to the end and, when correcting the dog for a move or an intention to move, keep your body posture upright.

After two or three days you can go into the next stage where you get further away from your dog. Hold the handle of the leash in your left hand at about waist height. When you give him the command and signal to stay you will be able to move away

77

Above: Fig. 42. If the dog starts to move, quickly correct by stepping forward to give a jerk above his head. Do not bend over but keep upright to hold his attention. *Right:* Fig. 43. When returning to his side by going around his back, keep your left hand in front of his nose while you revolve around him

much further, letting the leash hang down under his chin (fig. 41). Continue to walk around in a frontal semi-circle but do not attempt to go around his back. This will come later. For the time being it is essential for him to keep his attention on you, and to build up confidence in remaining calm and still on that spot. If he starts to move, step forward and give a jerk on the leash with your right hand above his head (fig. 42).

After a few more days, provided all is going well with this sit-stay, you can do more of them, for slightly longer periods of time and now start to return to his right side by going around the back of him. His natural reaction will be to watch you as you walk around him, and this is likely to cause him to move. To avoid this keep your left hand (which is holding the leash) in front of his nose (fig. 43). This will keep his attention to the front while you walk

close and around the back of him at normal speed. Before he knows what has happened you are standing beside him. You have in fact revolved around your left hand. You will only need to do this a few times and he will be quite happy about it. Soon you will be able to return around the back of him without holding your hand in front of him.

Remember that in order to get the best results always lay a good foundation in the first place. Matters such as working for extended durations of time, or at a long distance, walking around the back of him, and finally going completely out of sight will all come later. I have had some dogs who were very disturbed if I went around behind them. I had to leave this stage for several weeks, but in the meantime a solid foundation was being laid. Then finally those dogs did not mind where I was. All dogs are different. What you can do with some you cannot always do with others. Never rush it, take it steadily, and be patient with your dog.

11

The Recall

The recall is the most important exercise in dog training. Without it you cannot advance any further. You will never be able to trust your dog off the leash and you will never be able to train your dog to do retrieving, scent discrimination, jumping, tracking, and other advanced exercises.

It is an exercise which needs to be taught as early as possible. So as soon as you have trained your dog to do simple heel work, and the sit-stay, do not waste any time before teaching him the recall on the leash. Other exercises like the stand and down can wait. When clients come to me for training once a week I believe in teaching them how to recall their dogs in the third lesson.

Let us assume that your dog can now do the sit-stay exercise. Give him the command 'Stay', turn around in front of him and face him, walk backwards for a metre or so, and halt. The leash, with handle in your left hand, should be quite slack (fig. 44). If it is even a little tight it may cause him to get up and come before he is called. Stand there for a few seconds; then command him positively yet with an inviting tone 'Shane, come'. It may be necessary to bend

down and pat your knee with your other hand if he needs further encouragement when you call him. As soon as he responds by standing up and moving his first paw towards you, say 'Good dog' and keep praising him as you walk slowly backwards (fig. 45). As you do so gather in the leash so that he does not trip over it, but do not pull it tight. You are not hauling in a shark on the end of a line! When you have gathered it in, give him the command 'Sit' as you stop still, pull the leash up vertically over his head into your chest, and at the same time push his hindquarters down and towards you with your other hand (fig. 46). Immediately praise him as he responds. In order to get the best results at this point, praise very gently with both hands on either side of his face (fig. 47).

Keep talking to him and hold your head up as high as you can. All this will continue to capture his attention and he should look straight up to your eyes. Remain in this position for a short time to impress upon him that he has to come to face the front of your body. It is most important that you face in this direction from the time you call him to the time you sit him in front of

Left: Fig. 44. *The Recall on the Leash* Command him to 'Stay', leave him, and keep his attention. *Right:* Fig. 45. *The Recall* Command him 'Shane, come'. Immediately the dog responds praise him, walk backwards slowly, and gather in the leash without pulling it tight

you. Walk backwards in a very straight line. If he attempts to go off it, say 'Come' again and give him the necessary jerk on the leash which will bring him back on to that straight line. Do not forget to praise him the instant he returns on to the line, even though you have jerked him into that position. He will soon learn that if he comes straight he will be praised, but if he wanders off he will receive the necessary correction. When you have completed this exercise, return to his right side, take him forward at heel for a few metres, and then carry out another recall. You could do as many as

three of these with a little heel work after each one.

You will notice that this is all kept within the principle of the straight line concept. One of the best places you can practise keeping in a straight line while doing this is on a footpath. Training your dog on the streets has a further advantage. You are training him among distractions—people walking by, children playing, stray dogs, traffic, and many other things. But for the first couple of days it is best to teach him the recall on the leash in a quiet area, and then when he has got the idea of it you can

Fig. 46. *The Sit*   Pull the leash up vertically and push his hindquarters down and towards you if it is necessary

take him to areas where there are a few distractions.

When you get to this stage of training you need to be very careful that you do not do too many recalls in succession. If you do, within a very short time your dog will expect to be called every time you leave him. He is then likely to anticipate the command and get up. You cannot blame him really. He is using his initiative to make the next movement, but, in fact, he is disobeying the command 'Stay'. It is your training procedure which is wrong, so what you need to do is as follows. Start by giving him some heel work and include say two sit-stays. Then do a little more heel work followed by three or four recalls. More heel work with one or two sit-stays. Another few minutes of heel work followed by a few more recalls, and so on. By breaking it up you will prevent your dog getting bored and by putting in sit-stays now and then you will keep your dog guessing as to whether you are going to call him or return to him after you have told him to stay.

When you feel that your dog understands what 'Come' means you will be able to start doing recalls off the leash in a safe enclosed area. Try doing one on the leash and then immediately do another off the leash. Carry out the same procedure a few minutes later—one recall on the leash and one off the leash. Provided that all goes well, gradually reduce the number of recalls on the leash as his daily training progresses. If at any time he runs off when doing a recall off the leash, when you have caught him always take him back to the same spot and repeat the recall on the leash. You cannot afford to have this happen again, and by having him on the leash you will be able to uphold your command if necessary.

Even when you have taught your dog the basic recall, numerous faults can develop and, if not corrected, they become bad habits.

Many young dogs are very exuberant and, when called, come so fast that they either run past their trainer or even knock him over! If this happens with your dog, shorten the distance of the recall to give yourself better control. You will be able to say 'Sit' just before he reaches you and if you get your timing right you should have him sitting just in front of your feet. Much depends on the speed at which he is running when you give the command, how you say it, and the time it takes him to react in putting on the brakes. You will have to work these things out yourself.

If he does run past you, do not turn around to face him, otherwise he is likely to run rings around you, literally. Instead, keep your body facing the same way as it was when you first called him, and walk forward in that direction, calling him again over your shoulder. He should then run after you. Just as he passes you again, walk backwards a few steps, saying 'Shane, come', and sit him in front of you. Do not hesitate to use your hands to sit him if you find it necessary to do so. In this correction you have maintained the straight line, you have shown your dog that you were not going to turn to him, and in correcting him you have stepped in the opposite direction to where he was going.

Another way of slowing up a very fast dog is to have a wall or fence behind you. Although this is regarded as an artificial means of correcting a fault like this, it is of value when training some dogs. Obviously the dog will slow up—his instinct of self preservation will tell him that he will hurt himself if he does not. But do not have your back right up against the wall or fence, because he may sit crookedly when he comes to you, and you will not be able to

Left: Fig. 47. Praise with both hands and keep upright so that the dog looks straight up at you

step back any further to re-sit him straight in front of you. So when you use this method, have about a metre between your back and the wall. This will give you room to step back to make any minor adjustments such as correcting crooked sits.

Other dogs can be quite the opposite — they lack willingness and are slow. Some of them are so lazy that they are quite content to sit there and not come at all.

The first thing you need to do is to lengthen the recall distance by walking away in an irregular zig-zag fashion, facing the dog all the time. When you leave him in this way he should show more interest because he will be curious about your odd movements. By lengthening the distance you will have a better chance of making him anxious to reach you. Call him and praise lavishly. You can always run backwards a bit more, which will often excite him to come in faster.

Another method is to call your dog and instantly fall flat on your face. He should get such a surprise that he will race to find out what has happened to you. As he does so give him joyful praise and then slowly stand up as he is about to reach you. Then more praise.

Another common fault in the recall is when dogs come too far over to the left or the right. One of the reasons for this is because the finish to the recall has been taught too early and consequently when the dog comes he decides to do the finish all in one. Because we in Australia have to finish our dogs by getting them to heel around our backs to our left sides, many dogs when recalled tend to come over to our right. It is interesting to note, however, that in England and many other countries dogs are allowed to finish either as we do or by swinging around directly to the left side. This is done by using the method explained in Chapter 8 on how to do a left-about turn. Dogs which do this type of finish are likely to come over to the left when recalled.

To prevent this fault developing introduce the finish very gradually. To start with, out of every four recalls only include a finish with one of them, preferably the last one. Then try it with one in every three recalls, later every other one and finally every recall. This is the best way of maintaining the straight line approach your dog should make in the recall.

To correct this fault which has developed, firstly, cease doing the finish, or only do it on very few occasions for the next week or so. Secondly, when you see your dog deviate from the straight line as he does his recall, side-step in the opposite direction. You can lean right over, extending one leg and your arm in that direction. As you do this, emphasise the word 'Come'; then as soon as he comes on to a line straight in front of you praise him and walk backwards a few steps, encouraging him in straight towards you.

It is quite wrong for you to side-step in the direction the dog deviates to, as he would then expect you always to go to meet him.

The correction to the right-bowed recall is shown in fig. 48.

With all these faults you should move in the opposite direction to that of your dog, but on no account should you turn your body; always remember to keep facing the original direction.

The Finish

Many years ago the common method of bringing a dog around to heel after it had come and sat in front of you, was to say 'Heel' and give him a series of little jerks on the leash. This gradually brought him around the back of his owner until he was

Fig. 48. *How to Correct a Right-Bowed Recall*   In this instructional picture, the handler follows, in mirror-like fashion, the signals from his instructor by leaning over in the opposite direction to which his dog is bowing out in the recall

told to sit as he reached his owner's left side. The dogs did the exercise satisfactorily, but many did it with some reluctance because they had to be repeatedly jerked into this position.

Then another method was introduced without any jerks. The trainer would say 'Heel', take a full pace backwards with his right foot, and give an additional enticement with his right hand (which held the leash). The dog would respond by moving forward. As soon as he had moved the distance, the trainer would bring his right foot forward again and at the same time pass the leash from his right to his left hand behind his back; he would then turn his head around to his left side and say 'Heel' again. The dog would do a right-about turn, follow the direction of the voice and walk forward to sit at his trainer's left side.

This was a fairly good method, but it produced one fault. The dog developed the pattern of walking wide around his trainer because the trainer put his right foot back.

Now I have always believed that when a fault occurs you must in most cases carry out an opposite action to correct the fault. So I decided to work on a better method for the finish to the recall. Instead of stepping backwards, I tried stepping forwards with both feet (moving the right foot first) close to the dog's right side. I passed the leash from right to left hand behind my back and, turning my head to the left and under my arm, said, 'Heel'. The dog naturally thought I was going for a walk in that direction and his instant desire was to join me. In so doing he followed the direction from which my voice came and immediately came to my left side in the shortest distance and time (figs 49–52). I was very pleased with this, for it was the response I wanted.

The dog sitting in front of his handler

The handler steps forward with his right foot, straight and close to his dog

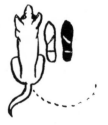

As the left foot is taken close to the right foot the handler commands his dog 'Heel' and then 'Sit' at his side

Fig. 49. Finish to the Recall

Left: Fig. 50. *The Finish* To teach him how to come to heel, step forward, turn your head to the left, and call him 'Heel'. *Centre:* Fig. 51. The dog seeing you go in that direction will be eager to join you. *Right:* Fig. 52. As soon as the dog reaches your side you sit him and praise

I tried this out on a team of six guide dogs which I was training at that time and, when I felt that they understood this first stage of the exercise, I took only half a pace forward with both feet. Then, later only a quarter of a pace forward, and finally I made no movement and the dogs responded perfectly to just the command 'Heel'. The results were most gratifying for all the dogs came to heel closely and willingly and without a jerk being given. The results were as good as those seen when training the puppy to finish with the use of meat as explained in Chapter 2.

A dog which breaks from the sit-stay or runs away when you call him has a lack of or no respect for you. It can happen with any of us at any time. It is something that we all have to accept, but at the same time we must always take immediate steps to correct such a fault.

When your dog runs away, you should always call him and run in the opposite direction first. If this fails, you must go after your dog, put him on the leash, return to the same place, and teach him on the leash again. Just before you do you can give him about one minute's intensive heel work, with rapid turns and quick sits. This will help to regain that respect he should have for you.

However, some dogs will only run off when you call them from a distance and this is where the check-cord method can

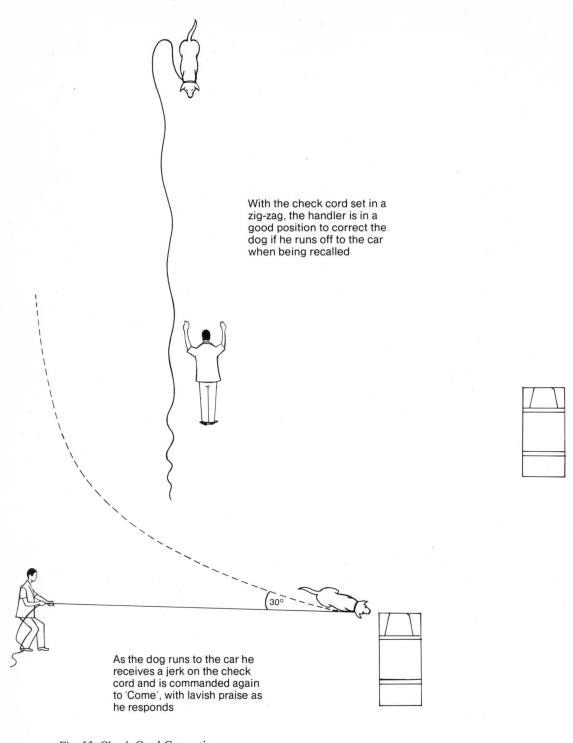

With the check cord set in a zig-zag, the handler is in a good position to correct the dog if he runs off to the car when being recalled

30°

As the dog runs to the car he receives a jerk on the check cord and is commanded again to 'Come', with lavish praise as he responds

Fig. 53. Check Cord Correction

be used to correct the dog. It needs careful planning and correct timing if you are to succeed.

This cord should be strong, at least 10 metres long, and have a strong snap hook on the end of it. You should set it out in a zig-zag fashion on the ground on the opposite side to where you reckon he will run off (fig. 53). For example he may run towards your car because he knows that if he can get inside he will not have to do any more work. Sit him at the clip end of the check cord, put it on discreetly, and make quite a show about taking your leather leash off him. Tell him to stay, walk away to a point near to the other end of the check cord, call him, and praise him as soon as he comes towards you. If, however, he runs off, pick up your end of the check cord, brace yourself, and call him again when he has nearly got to the full length of the cord. At this point, jerk him. He will probably roll over when you do this as he may be running fairly fast. The jerk will be unpleasant and quite unexpected by him. Drop the check cord immediately to show him that you have had nothing to do with it, and that it was some other outside force which jerked him! Call him again with lavish praise. He should be only too happy to join you. By a method of trial and error he will have found that it is going to be an extremely unpleasant sensation to run away from you, but a very pleasant one to come to you.

Ideally the angle at which you jerk him should be about thirty degrees to his body. You should also fix it so that as he runs off he does not get the check cord under his legs. So when you say 'Stay' to him ensure that the cord is lying down his back or well back to his side. The reason for setting the check cord out in a zig-zag fashion is so that your end of it will remain still for a few seconds while he is running away, enabling you to pick it up. Grip it very hard and even wear gloves, otherwise the cord might burn your hands if it slips through at speed.

If this corrective method is done with accuracy, it is often only necessary to do it once in the dog's lifetime. Many dogs have been cured once and for all of running off, but in using it trainers have had to be precise in their timing of giving the correct action and vocal control.

12

Stand and Stand for Examination

The stand is one of the easiest exercises to teach a dog, and you may wonder why we do not teach this exercise first. There are two reasons. Firstly, the sit is considered far more important, as you will have realised from reading previous chapters. Secondly, the dog is more likely to move in the stand position when told to stay, whereas he is more stable in the sit position.

To teach your dog the stand have him walking at heel on the leash. Prepare to stand him by taking hold of the leash (very close to the clip) in your right hand. Give him the command 'Stand' and give a quick horizontal backward jerk along his right shoulder. At the same time place your left hand on the front of his left hind leg, and lock it back (fig. 54). He will be less likely now to go into the sit position. Immediately you have carried out these simultaneous actions relax the leash and take your left hand away to praise your dog. Keep your feet facing straight and in line with the dog's forelegs. Give the command 'Heel' and go forward again to do more stand stops.

Having taught your dog the meaning of the word 'Stay' (in Chapter 9) you will now be able to apply it with this stand position.

It is my belief that the dog learns the stand, partly instinctively and partly in training. A similar action can be seen when a dog mates a bitch. His front paws will lock around in front of her hind legs, and the bitch will, in most cases and if she is ready, stand instinctively. What you are doing then with your left hand action gets a similar response. But you may think that this would only work in the case of a bitch. Surprisingly enough it works with male dogs as well. In kennels which have large numbers of dogs and bitches in the exercise runs it is not uncommon to see bitches mounting bitches and dogs mounting dogs.

Stand for Examination
With very sound dogs which are taught to stand and stay, there are no problems when the time comes for the dog to be examined by someone, particularly the judges in obedience trials or shows. However, many dogs have slight nervous troubles (just like their owners) when competing in the ring! These dogs' nerves seem to get worse when they are told to stay and be manhandled by a stranger.

To prevent this fault developing, dogs

should be brought up to a person who is going to examine them. The dogs should be allowed to move around in an area of independence. By moving about in this relaxed way they will not feel under a strict obligation to stand stay. As the days and weeks go by, dogs should become accustomed to being handled and their fears should melt away. During these weeks the stand stay should be taught without them being examined.

Finally, when you feel that your dog is happy about being handled and he knows how to stand stay, you can put the two together and you will have stand for examination.

Unfortunately many dogs are put off by the examiner (often a dog club instructor) approaching the dog. It is important that the examiner stays where he is and asks the owner to approach with the dog. Later, the examiner can make a very short approach which can gradually be lengthened.

Dogs who are timid and who get behind their owners, very much like shy children hiding behind their mother's skirts, should be prevented from doing so. Although it is a form of basic nervousness, this seeking for security can become a habit. So if your dog does this, keep facing to the front and, with your left hand on the clip end of the leash, bring the dog around to your left side, or slightly in front if you like, let go, and praise him. On no account turn round or let your dog achieve getting behind you. He has got to learn to stand literally on his own four feet.

Apart from many people bringing their dogs to me for obedience training every week, there are others who come with problems they are having with their dogs in the show ring. Most of the problems are caused by the owners having their dogs on tight leashes. They do this to hold their dogs

Fig. 54. *The Stand*   Command 'Stand' and jerk horizontally on a very short leash and lock the left hind leg back

heads up and sometimes to hide other faults the dogs may have. I am very glad to see that more and more judges are asking exhibitors to show their dogs on slack leashes. When a dog is on a tight leash he can start to worry. I have seen dogs held up so tightly that they have been gasping for air; some have even snapped at the judge when being examined. One lady brought me two Weimaraners who would shut their eyes and more or less go to sleep standing up. I told her to slacken her tight

93

leash and the dogs' eyes opened and remained open.

Many people in the show ring are under the impression that show work and obedience do not mix. I believe they can, in fact they should complement each other.

Many of the small breeds show shyness when approached by a judge who appears to be towering above them. These shy dogs can gain much confidence in training if they are examined by people sitting at a table where they are down to the dog's level (fig. 55).

It is a wonderful sight to see a dog gait on a loose leash, to stand on command, and show alertness in holding his head up. This can be achieved by giving him basic obedience and by getting his attention to look up at you (fig. 56). If you wish to crouch down, your show dog will feel more relaxed if you hold his head up with one finger under his chin (fig. 57) so that he

Below: Fig. 55. Many shy dogs gain confidence when you get down to their level. Later they will not mind examiners towering over them. *Right:* Fig. 56. Rather than hold a show dog's head up with a very tight leash, it is better to get his attention with your upright position

can breathe easily, instead of holding his head up with a tight leash.

It would not be right for me to finish this chapter without a word to people who examine dogs, particularly the judges.

From time to time I am very surprised and most concerned to see the way they march straight up to strange dogs in the ring and lay heavy hands on them without letting the dogs sniff their hands first. In the show ring it is true that they have to put a little pressure on the dogs' hindquarters to judge how stable they are, but even so, this is very often overdone.

I don't think many judges stop to realise that an incorrect action on their part can be harmful to a dog's temperament in the future. When this happens owners can feel heartbroken, especially when they have spent much time, care, and money on their pets.

Some obedience trial judges have been known to press far too hard on dogs, and this naturally causes them to move and consequently lose points. The judge in an obedience trial is there to judge the dog's temperament, and he should just run his hands over the dog quite gently. He will soon be able to judge a dog's temperament this way. There are some dogs which have been injured at some time or another and obviously such spots can be sensitive. So those who judge at obedience trials should be very considerate and remember what they are judging the dog for. I always think that it is a great shame when clients come to my school with dogs which have been frightened due to incorrect handling by those who have examined them in the show ring.

It often takes weeks and months to get the confidence of these dogs restored, and this can only be done by patient, careful handling and a quiet reassuring voice.

Fig. 57. A show dog will feel more relaxed if you hold his head up with one finger under his chin instead of holding it up tight by the collar

13

The Drop

This exercise can really be taught at any stage, and there are several ways of teaching it. If one method does not work there are usually a few more which you can try.

If you have a very difficult dog, I would be inclined to teach him all the other exercises first, i.e., those exercises which I have explained up until now. By doing it this way you will have gained a lot of respect from your dog. You will then find that teaching him to drop, which is also known as the down, will be much easier than if you started this exercise too early, when he may rebel against going down.

Assuming your dog is fairly easy to control, you could teach him this exercise at any stage and it is quite a good idea to do it at another time of the day, completely outside his daily training session. For instance, you could teach him this indoors on a comfortable carpet every day. It is an exercise which you can do in a confined space and for short periods of time during the television commercial breaks.

The first method is the one I explained in Chapter 2 when training a puppy. If your adult dog has forelegs which are too thick for you to put your fingers around, you can pass your right forearm under his right leg and take hold of his left leg. You will find this easy if you face the side of your dog and kneel down on your right knee. Do not forget to place your left hand on his shoulders and push down as you lift his forelegs (fig. 58).

If this method fails, try holding a very short leash directly under the dog's neck. Say 'Drop' or 'Down', jerk straight down to the ground with your right hand, simultaneously pushing down on your dog's shoulders with your left hand (fig. 59).

Another method you can use, and this depends upon the size of your dog, is to take his right foreleg in your right hand and his left in your left hand. Command him to drop; lift both his legs upwards and as you do so press on his shoulders with your left elbow.

The easiest method of all, provided your dog is curious enough, is to pat the ground with your right hand at a point just below his nose. Some dogs will just lie down because they are curious to see what you are doing. If this is the case, consider yourself very lucky that your dog will oblige in this way.

Left: Fig. 58. *The Drop*   With your left hand on his shoulders, pass your right arm under his right foreleg and take hold of his left leg. Command 'Drop' and lift his legs at the same time as you push his shoulders down. *Right:* Fig. 59. *The Drop—an alternative method*   Command 'Drop', jerk down on a short leash, and push on his shoulders. With both methods, immediately the dog responds praise him by stroking him under the chin

Once I had to train a St Bernard to lie down and found that by just lifting one of his forelegs (the size of which was like the leg of a small pony) he went straight down, as he could not support his great weight on the other leg. You never know your luck sometimes.

It has also been known for some trainers to say 'Down' whenever they saw a dog just about to lie down naturally. Although this can take a long time and you need to be with your dog a lot, he can learn in this way. This method of training is one where an instinctive action is coupled with a training command.

When you use any of these methods you must praise the dog as soon as he hits the ground. It is a good idea to praise him physically *under* the chin with your right hand. This will be an incentive for him to want to lie down and stay there, whereas in the sit and stand exercises it is best to stroke the dog on top of the head so as to attract his head upwards.

The drop is easier to teach from the sit position, because you have his hindquarters on the ground already. When he understands the meaning of the word 'Down' or 'Drop', it can be given when you are working him in heel work. Your right hand action on his forelegs will gradually become a hand signal for this exercise. If you want to maintain accuracy, always bring your right hand straight down like a guillotine in front of your dog's nose. If you sweep your hand action down and away from him, he may lie out too far ahead. If you sweep it down and across in front of your feet, he is likely to lie down across you. The reason for these two faults is that he simply follows your hand. While he is learning to drop during heel work, you want to have your left hand just above his shoulder, so that you can uphold your command by pushing him down, without any hesitation, if he does not respond straight away.

Some dogs, when made to lie down, roll over and then want to play. As soon as you see this happen, straighten yourself up. In most cases a dog will then lie up properly when he sees you straighten up and act very seriously. If you tend to crouch down and over your dog, he may think that you are going to tickle his tummy and will naturally roll over on his back. As I have mentioned before, dogs recognise our body positions and associate these with other things we have done with them in the same positions at different times.

In training your dog to perform the down stay you should apply the same procedure as applied to the stay in the sit or stand position, viz., make sure he fully understands the exercise before you attempt to go too far away, or before you prolong the exercise for extended periods of time.

From time to time you may hear some trainers say that the down exercise should be one of the very first which you teach your dog, because you will get out of him a total submission. I personally condemn this idea. I believe that you should teach your dog to lie down just like you teach him to do any other exercise—so that he does it willingly and respects you as the firm and loving master.

There is nothing worse than to see a dog working in a fearful sort of way, with his head and tail down and looking utterly dejected.

People who train these dogs are always far too hard on them and use poor and callous methods of training. Such methods for teaching the down may include stamping quickly on the clip end of the leash to force the dog down, or quickly bowling the dog over while he is trotting along at heel. The former is unpleasant to the dog and shows laziness on the part of the trainer, who in my opinion should not be training the dog at all if he can't be bothered to get down and teach him properly so that he likes doing it. The latter way can be most disturbing to the dog and will in most cases be very inaccurate. The dog may go down, but in doing so is likely to move away and come to rest at an angle.

So remember, teach him to drop down so well that he likes doing it, and not just to get a total submission from him.

14

The Retrieve

The retrieve exercise is the stepping stone to advanced work. It should be introduced gradually, but at an early age. Some breeds, such as Labradors, Golden Retrievers, and those used for gun-dog work, retrieve instinctively, (although you will occasionally find a dog among these breeds who will not retrieve). There are other breeds which, although they do not do it instinctively, are very adaptable when it comes to being trained to retrieve. Finally, there are a few breeds, like the Chow Chow, which neither do it instinctively nor are adaptable to retrieving, and this is something we just have to accept.

In obedience trials throughout the world the wooden dumb-bell is the recognised article the dog has to retrieve. While many dogs can easily be taught to hold, carry, and fetch these dumb-bells, others do not readily take to it. With these dogs it is best to start off with something else which they like to retrieve. I have found that something light and soft is best. A piece of rolled up leather in the shape of a tube, an old leather glove, or a disused pair of socks neatly turned into each other will do. Pick a time of day when your dog is very lively, and

have him in an enclosed area where there are no distractions.

The first method you should try is mysteriously to talk and play with the article by passing it slowly around your legs. You can say in a very quiet and inviting tone, 'What's this, Rex? What is it? Would you like this? Oh! Where's it gone?' If he is interested in what you have, he will watch it go behind your legs and then see it reappear. His interest will often increase and he will go after it. As he is just about to take hold of it, say 'Hold', and as soon as he takes it in his mouth say 'Good dog'. If you walk backwards, inviting him to come, he should do so. As he reaches you take hold of the article and say 'Give', and as soon as he releases his grip say 'Good dog'. If by any chance he holds on to it, do not pull because he will only grip it harder and you will end up in a tug-of-war, and the next time he gets it he will probably run off with it. Instead, release his grip by putting a finger in the corner of his mouth and remove the article with the other hand.

Many adult dogs need to have their interest aroused even more so. If your dog is one of these put him on a leash and take him out on the lawn. Start playing with the wooden dumb-bell or article, keeping it up high (fig. 60). Throw it up about half a metre in the air and catch it again. Keep turning around and while you are doing this talk to him in a very excitable and interesting tone. Give him the impression that the article is yours, and that he cannot have it. A dog's interest will often increase by watching it, and he should then run around you to get it, and finally leap up to grab it. As he leaps up for it say 'Hold' (fig. 61) and as he takes hold of it say 'Good dog' (fig. 62).

When he reaches the stage that his interest is really aroused toss it on the ground about a metre in front of him (fig. 63). He should seize the opportunity to pounce on it. At this point you must praise him and call him towards you and take it from him. Try it once again and he should love getting it. It becomes a great game to him. Only do it two or three times and no more. If you overdo it, he will get bored and lose interest forever. Put the article back in your pocket, or in a top drawer, or anywhere where he cannot get it. You have to convey the impression that it is something very special, something which is brought out for special occasions.

If these methods do not work, then you will just have to show him how to hold it by opening his mouth and putting it in. Have him on the leash, sitting at heel. Place the leash under your foot. This will stop him if he tries to walk away, and will leave you both your hands free. Stroke his head slowly with your left hand and put it over his muzzle. Having the dumb-bell or article in your right hand, put your little finger of your right hand into the corner of his mouth. As he opens it feed the article into his mouth, saying 'Hold' and 'Good dog' (fig. 64). It may be necessary to keep his

Fig. 60. *The Retrieve* 'Would you like this?' Many dogs will show interest if the dumb-bell is kept high and the handler teases the dog with it

mouth shut, but not too tightly. Use one hand for this and praise him gently with the other. Only leave it in his mouth for about two seconds and then remove it. Repeat this two or three times only, and then let him go free with much lavish praise.

After a few days, or when he has reached the stage of holding it without rebellion, see if he will take it when you hold it about one centimetre in front of his nose. When

Above: Fig. 61. As he leaps up for it say 'Hold'. *Top right:* Fig. 62. As he takes hold of it say 'Good dog'. *Bottom right:* Fig. 63. When his interest is really aroused toss it on to the ground and he should seize the opportunity to pick it up and carry it

he does, praise him immediately with your voice and stroke him very slowly, with the back of your fingers, just between his eyes and back towards the top of his head (fig. 65). You should find this very effective in getting him to keep his head up. You will also find that when he holds his head up he will be less likely to drop the article. If you stroke him under his chin, he may tend to lower his head and drop the thing.

When he has reached the stage of taking it, you can gradually hold it a little bit further away from him and lower to the ground. Of course you do not want to have him in the sitting position for this, as you are expecting him to move forward to take hold of it. So let him just stand relaxed beside you.

As the days go by, you should soon reach the stage when he will take it from your hand when it is resting on the floor. Then start tossing it a metre or so away and tell him to 'Hold' or 'Fetch'. Don't worry about sitting him first or when he comes back with it, or doing a finish. Just get him happy and enthusiastic about going out for it, picking it up, and bringing it back to you. All the other things can be included later.

If you are using a piece of leather, glove or sock, when you feel that he likes picking up this article try binding it around a piece of dowling or broomstick about 15 centimetres long. This will now be a little heavier and more solid. Then at a later stage add two square blocks of wood to the ends and you will have a dumb-bell. He should take hold of the centre part, which he has become accustomed to over the days or weeks you have been training him.

This method can be used successfully on a dog who retrieves, but continuously takes hold of either end of the dumb-bell instead of the centre. If he picks up

Above: Fig. 64. *The Retrieve—an alternative method* With your left hand over his muzzle put the dumb-bell into his mouth, saying 'Hold'. *Below:* Fig. 65. Praise the dog lightly on top of the head with the back of your fingers. This will help him to keep his head up and hold on to the dumb-bell

any articles by either end, it will be unbalanced and he is likely to drop it because the weight tends to turn his head on one side. Apart from this being a training fault, it can also be penalised in obedience trials. In most cases this fault develops from bad training in the first place. If this is so, it is always best to go back to the beginning and start again. This principle not only applies to the retrieve but to other exercises as well.

Another common fault found in retrieving is mouthing. This can lead to a dog chewing the article, dropping it, or even tossing it in the air and catching it.

One way to correct this is to give the dumb-bell or article to the dog and immediately do some heel work at a brisk pace in a clockwise direction. In the vast majority of cases you will find that your dog will concentrate better as he has to keep up with you, and because he has to concentrate more he will cease to mouth the article. Do not go around in an anti-clockwise direction as you may walk into him or accidentally knock the article out of his mouth. You will also need to ensure that the leash does not touch the dog's face as this may cause him to drop the article.

Another way is to stand near the corner of a building; throw the dumb-bell and tell him 'Fetch'. As he picks it up, call him and hide just around the corner. He will be very anxious to race back to you and you will find that he will not even think about mouthing it. As he comes around the corner praise him and take the article. Do not trouble about making him sit, just take it before he starts mouthing again. As soon as you have overcome this mouthing you can introduce, or reintroduce, the sit in front of you and, of course, the finish.

Two other methods can be used. One is to make the dumb-bell heavier, which will make the dog grip it more and hang on to it; the other is to give the dog a little tap with your hand under his chin every time he starts to mouth it. As you do this say 'Hold', and as he responds say 'Good dog'. I must warn you, however, that these two methods will only work with certain dogs, usually the tough ones. Remember that what will work for some may not necessarily work with others.

The most important point to remember throughout the retrieve training is never, never to tell your dog off when he drops the article. You could regard this principle as an exception to the rule. Up till now you have corrected him for all sorts of things by saying 'No', and you have possibly given a physical correction as well, but in the retrieve you should always repeat the exercise by showing him what you want him to do, and then praising him as he responds.

A young man once came to me with a problem he had with his dog. The dog had been retrieving well for several weeks and then one day for some reason or other he dropped the dumb-bell after he had picked it up. From then on he would not pick it up at all. I asked the owner what he did when his dog dropped it on that first occasion. He told me that he immediately yelled 'No!' and 'Pick it up'. The dog did not pick it up, but just stood there quite worried and confused. If you study the dog's mind for a moment, you will see that he associated the very severe vocal correction with picking up the dumb-bell and bringing it back, not with his act of dropping it. From then on every time he was told to 'Fetch' he expected to be corrected. What his owner should have done, was to have helped his dog by saying in a kind way 'Fetch it' and, if necessary, going and picking up the dumb-bell and encouraging the dog to hold it, giving immediate praise upon response. This would then have been a pleasurable experience. The dog's confidence would have been restored and there would have been continuity in the training.

However, all was not lost. The owner realised his mistake when I explained this to him. He followed my advice and started from the beginning again, and his dog was soon retrieving successfully. He had learned by his mistake and knew never to correct his dog in that way again, but to help him instead.

This same principle should be applied to your dog, particularly when he is a puppy, even when he picks up one of your treasured possessions. Never tell him off, but just say 'Good dog! Come! There's a good dog'. He will know that you are pleased with him as he brings it to you. He will not understand that it is something which you do not want him to touch. As far as he is concerned, it is there for him to pick up. Blame yourself if you do not want him to get it—you should not have left it lying around in the first place.

A certain Golden Retriever which I was once training as a guide dog had a passion for retrieving. I took her into my home one day and within a few minutes she had brought into the kitchen one of our children's toys. I praised her as she gave it to me and within seconds she had brought me another one. Before long the kitchen was full of toys. I decided that this could not go on any longer. I followed her discreetly and discovered that she had found the toy cupboard open in an upstairs bedroom. The problem was soon solved by shutting the door.

I know of a family who own a Border Collie, and although he stays close to their house most of the time, he takes off on occasions to visit neighbours' homes which, like his, have no fences. For some reason or other he loves retrieving brooms of all shapes and sizes. He brings these home, much to the embarrassment of the family. They do not know which homes he has taken them from, and what the owners might say if they came to visit and spotted their brooms. The answer to this problem is to have the dog fenced in so that he cannot wander off.

There are two other faults which often arise in the later stages of retrieve training. They are found in the dog who anticipates the handler's command to fetch, and the dog who, anticipating the handler taking the dumb-bell, drops it at his feet.

If you have thrown your dumb-bell, and your dog breaks from your side to retrieve it before you give the command 'Fetch', do not correct him. Let him use his initiative to retrieve it and keep him happy. If you correct him as he dashes out to it, you are likely to destroy that initiative, and you cannot afford to do this.

To overcome the difficulty do another retrieve immediately, but this time discreetly hold on to his slip collar so that at the first sign of him trying to move forward you can say 'Sit' and 'Stay', and give him a little backward jerk. Wait a few seconds and then say 'Fetch'. As soon as he takes hold of the dumb-bell say 'Good dog', and 'Come'. Continue to praise him as he comes to you, just like you do in the recall; then say 'Sit' as he comes in front of you.

If you think that he will drop the dumb-bell as your hand descends, keep his attention with your voice, saying 'Hold', and at the same time keep one hand up near your face. As you do all this, discreetly run your other hand down the back of your leg, then bring it around in front of you at a height a bit lower than his chin and take the dumb-bell. Because he is looking steadfastly up at you he will not notice your other hand coming from underneath.

Further to everything I wrote in Chapter 6 concerning the dog's sense of sight, this is a good time to explain another point on that subject. While dogs have side vision very much like ours, their height and depth angles of viewing things are different. I am sure you have all seen dogs lie down with their chins on the floor. When you walk around in front of them you will see their eyes follow you from one side to the other without them moving their heads. You will also see them roll their eyes upwards (more or less at ninety degrees) as they watch you stand over them. They cannot however, look downwards at a steep angle because of the structure of their heads. By comparison we cannot look upwards at any great angle because of our foreheads. But we can look downwards at a very steep angle.

It is important to remember this fact about your dog's angle of vision because you can make use of it when taking a dumb-bell from him in this crafty way.

Many people who become interested in advanced training and therefore want their dogs to retrieve despair when they cannot get their dogs to do it. They cannot understand why their dogs will not retrieve a dumb-bell or other article and yet they will chase after a ball.

The ball, usually a tennis ball, is the whole trouble. The dog treats it as a toy. He loves to chase after it as it bounces along. He enjoys getting it, squeezing it, dropping it, and watching it bounce or roll along the ground.

If you want to teach your dog how to retrieve, do not use a ball. It encourages a dog to mouth it and to drop it. Apart from this a ball can be dangerous. Dogs have been known to die when balls have become stuck in their throats. Dog owners *always* believe in throwing balls for their dogs in order to give them exercise. In my opinion this is not necessary. Without knowing it you can over do it with a young dog, if you throw a ball too many times. He will be eager to go after it again and again. The next thing you know is that he will be utterly exhausted. If you want to let your dog have some exercise, take him for a free run in a park somewhere, and let him run off his excess energy in his own time. You will see when he has had enough. This way he will exercise himself naturally.

15

Jumping and Retrieve over the Jump

Nearly every dog enjoys jumping over obstacles of various shapes and sizes. It stimulates his willingness to work and it prevents him from becoming bored.

I always feel sorry for a dog when he is paced up and down for far too long doing basic heel work. He reaches the point where he is absolutely fed up with it all. If only his handler would occasionally give him some other activity, like the odd jump here and there, he would have something he could look forward to every day. Something he would thoroughly enjoy doing.

Jumping is an exercise which can be taught even in the early stages of training. It should not necessarily be left until the dog has reached one of the top classes, as is often seen in obedience dog training clubs today. While jumping is all right for an adult dog, it should not be taught to a young puppy as it could be harmful to his bone development.

However, when he has reached the age of about five months, there would be no harm in teaching him how to jump over the base board of a high jump. This is only about 25 centimetres high and it is enough to teach him how to go over an obstacle on

command. The main thing you want to teach him is the procedure, which, like many other things you teach him, will then become a pattern in his mind. The jumps can be increased in height and length much later when the pattern has been established and his bones are stronger and more developed to cope with this energetic activity.

High Jump

As happens with all other exercises you teach your dog, have him on the leash when you teach him how to jump. Remember, you must have control over him and he has to rely upon you to show him how you want him to do it.

The height of the jump should be low so that he can look over it and see the ground on the other side. This is important because he needs to see what he is going to land on. If the jump was higher than his head, he would probably try to go around the jump instead of over it. It is very important that he be confident and sure in what he is doing when going over any type of jump.

First Stage Walk him at heel up to the jump, holding the leash in your left hand. Keep it just slack and above his head, so that there will be no chance of it getting

107

Fig. 66. *The High Jump—1st stage* Take the dog over the jump on the leash, signal with the right hand as you say 'Over', and return over the jump using the same method

It is very important when teaching your dog to go over the high jump that you always get him to return over it. Later, when he understands how to retrieve, he will have to retrieve over the jump if you wish to compete with him in the open obedience trials.

When I came to Australia I noticed that a number of dogs in these trials went over the jump and picked up the dumb-bell all right, but then the fault came: instead of returning over the jump, they came back around the side of it. By doing this they immediately forfeited over half their marks for that exercise. I then discovered why they were coming around the side. During the training sessions at some of the obedience dog clubs, the dogs and handlers lined up behind each other and on the command from their instructor, who was standing at the jump, they went over the jump one by one. After each dog and handler had done this they returned by a circular route to form up at the end of the queue again. When all had had a go, another board was added to the high jump to increase its height, and the same procedure was followed. You can see the pattern that was being formed in the mind of every dog: after he had jumped he returned by going around the side of the jump.

In the early stages of high-jump training walk up to the jump; do not run at it. If you run and go over it yourself, your dog at the last second may go around the side of the jump. Your leash will then catch the upright post and possibly pull it over, and this will frighten your dog. If he becomes frightened, he will not feel like going near that jump again.

Second Stage When he knows what to do you can start to speed up as you approach the jump. At this stage you should act in the same way but only up to the point

under one of his legs as he jumps. Give the command 'Over' in a very joyful tone and step over the jump. As you do this give him a hand signal with your right hand in an upward movement in front of him (fig. 66). As he responds in going over the jump with you praise him and keep walking for a few metres, about turn, and return over the jump exactly as you did before.

when your first foot is about to go over the jump. As he jumps let out more leash and bring your foot back. At the same time say 'Good dog! Come! Over! Good dog!'. You will need to position yourself in the middle of the jump so that he comes directly to you (fig. 67). As he jumps, quickly walk backwards a few steps and tell him to sit in front of you. You can now see how you can employ the recall in this high-jump exercise, and you are now operating from one side of the jump only.

Third Stage Now that he has the pattern in his mind, and provided the rest of his obedience is satisfactory, try doing it off the leash. You can at the same time raise the height of the jump a little. Continue to use your right hand as a signal for him to go over the jump and remember to keep your arm high. This will help to entice him up and over. I have seen people use their heads too low (at the dog's level), and their dogs have just stopped to sniff at the jump thinking that there was something there for them. So remember to keep your hand signal high.

Fourth Stage Sit your dog about three metres from the jump. Tell him to stay, and position yourself about one metre from the jump and just a little to the right. Give him the command 'Over' in a very enthusiastic tone. Praise him as he is in mid-air, and call him when he lands on the other side. Praise him as he jumps back over again, positioning yourself about three metres from the jump on the place where you told him to stay. As soon as he lands on the ground follow this up with another command 'Come', and then 'Sit' just as he arrives at your feet. Praise him and get him to finish to heel.

All you have to do now is gradually to modify your position which you take up to send him over the jump. Within a few days

Fig. 67. *The High Jump—2nd stage* Still on the leash, the dog jumps over on his own and is recalled back over the jump

you will not even have to go one metre away from him towards the jump. Just have him sitting beside you, give him the command 'Over', and signal with your right arm. Excellent. He is finally doing the jump both ways while you remain quite still.

Retrieve over the jump
When you have taught your dog how to retrieve on the flat and how to jump, you

109

will find that teaching him to retrieve over the high jump is quite easy. However, to play safe it is always best to start this off from the beginning of stage four. Leave him at the sit, and position yourself up against the right-hand post of the jump. Hold your dumb-bell in your right hand. Command him 'Over' and, as he leaps, toss the dumb-bell to a distance of a few metres over the jump and say 'Fetch' (fig. 68). Praise as soon as he takes hold of it and call him back over the jump.

You need to time your throw of the dumb-bell well. It should be as he is in the act of leaping up. If you throw it too early he may run around the jump to fetch it. Although he has learned how to jump and retrieve in two separate exercises, he has now got to combine the two together. Gradually modify your position and it will not be long before you are doing it all from the one position without moving (fig. 69). Continue to use the two commands 'Over' and then 'Fetch' for a while. Eventually, just say 'Fetch'. He will then understand that he has got to fetch by going over the jump and returning the same way.

Do not worry about setting the jump too high. Make it easy for him to understand. When you really feel he knows the exercise thoroughly, you can then put up the height to one-and-a-half times his shoulder height (as laid down in the Australian Obedience Trials rules and regulations). It may be necessary to give your dog a little longer run at the jump as you make it higher. A lot depends on your dog's jumping ability.
Bar Jump
When a dog has been taught how to jump over a high jump, it is very easy to get him to go over the black and white bar of the bar jump (fig. 70). He is not required to retrieve over this bar in the obedience trials, but it comes in the exercise of direc-

Fig. 68. *Retrieve over the High Jump*   The dumb-bell is released from the right hand as the dog leaps

tional jumping found in Chapter 21.

Start by taking your dog over the bar both ways, but set the bar at such a height that he cannot run under it. He will learn this very quickly and as he does you can gradually raise the height until it is one-and-a-half times his shoulder height.
The Broad Jump
In Chapter 6 I wrote about the dog's sense

of vision and mentioned that because he sees life at a lower level the third dimension is difficult for him to judge.

You have only got to get down to his level and look at the broad jump from the direction in which you want him to jump over it and you will see that it looks like a white platform. It would be quite wrong to attempt to get him to clear it straight away, even if you knew that he was capable of jumping across a 3-metre creek! He would probably jump on to the broad jump, expecting it to be a low grooming table.

You therefore need to teach him how to jump one board first. Then two, three, and four put close together. Later they can be spaced out to the required distance. As laid down in the obedience trials rules and regulations, a dog is required to jump a distance equal to three times his shoulder height.

Right: Fig. 69. The handler stands in the centre and back from the high jump and recalls the dog over it. *Below:* Fig. 70. *The Bar Jump* In the early stages the dog should be taught to jump over the bar at a low height so that he cannot run under it. Gradually the height is increased

First Stage Trot up to the jump with your dog just as you did in stage one of the high jump. Jump over the right-hand end of it and, as he is trotting at heel with you, he will jump over the centre of the board. When he has jumped over he is required to come and sit in front of you before he completes the exercise with a finish to heel. To get him to do this, which is in fact a recall, as he is about to land on the ground, quickly say 'Come', side-step one pace to the right and then two steps to the rear. By doing this you will form a pattern in his mind and he will soon understand that as soon as he has cleared this broad jump he will have to right-about turn in a U shape and come to sit in front, facing you. In training you can either do a finish or go and stand beside him on his right. Then go forward with him at heel back to where you started the jump. I always do the latter in training to keep the continuity, and to prevent the dog anticipating the finish.

A fault often seen in training and obedi-

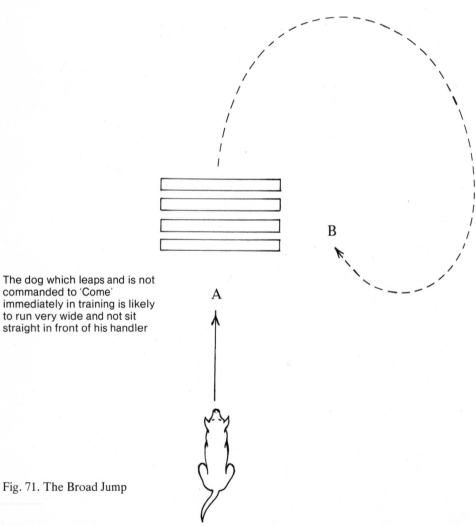

The dog which leaps and is not commanded to 'Come' immediately in training is likely to run very wide and not sit straight in front of his handler

Fig. 71. The Broad Jump

ence trials is where dogs jump so fast that they land well beyond the jump and bow out to the right (fig. 71).

In order to overcome this fault train your dog to come, as he lands. If you have him on the leash you can uphold your command and will therefore be able to guide him into the pattern you require. Another thing you can do is to have an imaginary line to the right of which you do not take the dog (fig. 72). The dog will soon learn that even after the exercise you are not going to go over that line into that area.

Second Stage Now that your dog has got the pattern, try doing it off the leash and with about three boards. Sit him a few metres from the jump and position yourself on the right side of it and facing it. Command 'Over' in a very enthusiastic tone, and at the same time give a quick upward and over hand signal. As he is in mid-air (and that it not for very long) command 'Come! Good dog!'. Turn to your right

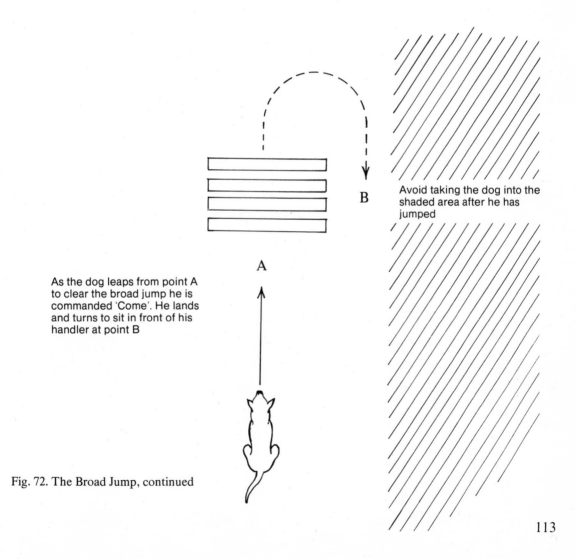

B

Avoid taking the dog into the shaded area after he has jumped

A

As the dog leaps from point A to clear the broad jump he is commanded 'Come'. He lands and turns to sit in front of his handler at point B

Fig. 72. The Broad Jump, continued

Above: Fig. 73. *The Broad Jump*   As the dog is about to land he is commanded to 'Come' and sit straight in front of the handler. *Below:* Fig. 74. *The Broad Jump*   As this dog jumps, the handler corrects the dog jumping diagonally by quickly putting one leg forward between the boards; this makes the dog jump straight

and, as he lands, encourage him to sit in front of you (fig. 73). Then finish. Well done. You have now taught him how to clear the broad jump.

There is another fault which often occurs and it is one which develops after the dog has been doing this jump for a while. You may find that he will start jumping at a slight angle to the right. He will do this because he anticipates the next part of the exercise, which is for him to turn and come to you. It also happens with a lazy dog who tries to cut off the corner.

This fault can be corrected very easily and quickly. As he runs towards the jump, step forward with one foot in between two of the boards (fig. 74). This will make him jump straight and not to the right. If you do this occasionally in training, it will always keep him guessing as to whether you are going to do it or not and this will make him play safe and jump straight. Here is another example of the principle: always be in a position to do something about it.

16

Advanced Heel Work

You have now reached a very important point in your dog's training. You have done all the elementary training on the leash, and now you must do it off the leash. You will soon know whether or not you have given your dog a good grounding in his basic training.

Advanced work includes automatic sits without commands; standing and dropping instantly on command and/or signal; heeling at normal, fast, and slow speeds; and working with fewer and fewer words of encouragement. It also demands much more concentration from your dog as he watches your body and foot movements in all the turns you make, including the figure eight. The first question many handlers ask is, 'When should I start heeling him off the leash?' The short answer to this is, 'When your dog heels perfectly on the leash.' This means that he should keep close beside you, obey all your commands, and not require any jerks or other physical actions to make him obey.

The next question is, 'How should I start doing it?' Obviously, like everything else in dog training, you should introduce it gradually and for short durations. Later these times can be extended until finally, after a few weeks, it can be done completely off the leash.

The best way to introduce it is to start off by doing a few minutes of heel work on the leash. Then about one minute off the leash. This could include a couple of right turns, two or three sits and a left turn. Now do a few more minutes of heel work on the leash. Then one minute off the leash with say a stand, a down, and a left-about turn. Once more back on the leash, and so on. If you follow this procedure, your dog should not get out of hand in the short periods off the leash, and when on the leash he will respect you as he has in the past.

During these times off the leash it is quite possible that he may wander too far to the left, do wide turns, lag, or even walk too far forward. If this occurs, put him back on the leash immediately. You will then have the means to uphold your commands and his respect for you will be restored.

Faults like these develop when handlers do not correct them quickly enough and go on, hoping for the best. Within a very short time the dog knows that he can get away with it. He loses respect for his owner and the training breaks down.

My advice to people as soon as they see faults like these arise is, do not just hope the situation will come right, do something about it—put him back on the leash. That is another training principle for you.

Automatic Sits

Many people say they have great difficulty in getting their dogs to sit without a command, or it has taken them months to perfect it.

Really it is quite simple. Provided the dog sits on command, take him to an open space where you can sit him four times in a straight line. Sit him first, say 'Heel', go forward two metres, and sit him again. Quickly praise. Forward again two more metres, sit him again on command. Quickly praise. Say 'Heel', go forward again for two metres, come to an abrupt halt, and he should sit without a command. As soon as he sits automatically, praise him. So in that distance of six metres he has sat four times. The first, second, and third sits were with the command 'Sit'. Because these were given rapidly within about nine seconds, it became a reflex action for the dog so that when the fourth sit came he sat automatically. The whole thing was done within about twelve seconds.

If the sits had been carried out with a distance of about ten metres between each one, then you would not have got the same effect. The training has to be rapid, within a short distance, and in a very short period of time. You can then walk on another fifty metres and do four more sits as before. Later you can reduce the number of sits to three, and say 'Sit' with the first and second only. Then try two rapid sits using a command with the first one only. Always be sure to praise him when he sits automatically in this stage of his training.

If at any time he does not respond then tell him to sit and make sure he does. I have often seen dogs in obedience trials standing beside their handlers when they should have been sitting. The handlers have said nothing, hoping or praying that their dogs would eventually sit. The dogs soon find out that they can get away with this in the ring. My advice to handlers who have this sort of trouble with their dogs in the ring is to say 'Sit' as soon as they see their dogs are not going to sit automatically. Naturally they will forfeit some of their points in giving this extra command, but they cannot afford to let the dog get away with it.

I learned this point from a very well-known trainer in England—Mrs Joan McMillan. She trained many dogs, including obedience champion Micklyn Shandy. Shandy was a cross-bred and won Crufts Obedience in 1970. Crufts is regarded as the top obedience competition in the country.

Joan always made a point of correcting any major errors her dogs made in the ring, even though it meant losing points. Minor errors, like slightly crooked sits, she did not bother to correct, unless she had already lost so many points that she was out of the running. She always looked to the future. Her dogs were brilliant, happy workers. She believed in praise where it was due, and correction wherever and whenever it was needed. With this principle foremost in her mind, it was not long before she was winning with very high marks, her dogs understanding and having the utmost respect and affection for her.

Dropping when heeling

If you have taught your dog the drop from the sit position, as in Chapter 13, and you feel that he really knows the meaning of the word 'Drop' or 'Down', you can now

117

teach him this while walking at heel.

Give him the command 'Drop' or 'Down' and bring your right hand straight down in front of him. It is a good idea always to have your left hand a couple of centimetres above his shoulders to push him down if he does not obey, or drops too slowly (fig. 75). A sudden push down from above will certainly make a dog go down quicker.

If he obeys instantly, try doing about four drops in a row, using a command and simultaneous hand signal with the first, second, and third drop. Then use the hand signal alone on the fourth drop. Like the automatic sits, do them with about two metres between each one. Do not forget to praise on all these, especially the last one where he has responded to a hand signal alone.

Standing when heeling

This can be taught in exactly the same way as the drop. Provided your dog stops instantly on command, it will not take long to teach him how to stand. Do about four stands in a row, and get him to do the last one by giving a hand signal only. The most common way of giving this hand signal is to bring your right hand around in a horizontal movement to the front of your dog's face. See fig. 78, page 133.

Slow pace in heel work

This is very easy when a dog has been taught everything at normal speed. Do not do too much of it though, if your dog tends to lag and show a lack of willingness.

In giving the command 'Heel' when you are about to step off at a slow speed, lower your voice and draw the command out a

Fig. 75. *Dropping a Dog in Heel Work*   Command 'Drop' and signal straight down with the right hand. To uphold the command and signal, the dog can be either jerked down with the right hand, or pushed down on the shoulders with the left hand

little. Not only will it keep a young excitable dog calm, but it will, in time, warn your dog at which speed you are going to go forward.

Fast pace in heeling

This is a speed in heel work which you should not attempt until you feel that you have absolute control over your dog. If your dog is young and has an excitable nature, running will increase this and he will soon get out of hand.

When you are about to go forward at a fast pace, you can warn him by raising the pitch of your voice as you say 'Heel'. It will not be long before he catches on to knowing at which speed you are going to move forward—just by the way you say 'Heel'.

Now there are two ways in which you can run. If you have a somewhat lethargic dog, you need to run like an elephant! Lift your legs high as you run to get him excited and you should find this will do the trick. On the other hand, if your dog is the very lively type, then you will need to run slowly and in a gliding manner which will help to keep him calm, so that he does not start jumping up at you.

Coming to a quick halt can often catch some dogs by surprise and they tend to overshoot. Try making very rapid footsteps as you bring yourself to a halt. You can exaggerate the sound of your footsteps by bringing your feet down harder. Give the command 'Sit' a fraction of a second earlier than you would if you were walking at normal pace. This method will give your dog a very good warning as to what you are going to do. As time goes on you can gradually leave off the command and become quieter and quieter as your rapid foot movements come to a halt.

Having taught your dog all this advanced heel work, your next question will probably be, 'When will my dog be ready for obedience trial work?' The short answer to this is, 'When you have trained your dog to work on and off the leash, to obey all the commands, to be reliable in the stays, and to be confident about being examined by the judge.' What you do in training you cannot necessarily do in obedience trials. The point you need to keep in mind is that, whichever method you use, or the way you go about training your dog, you should strive for the ultimate results with perfection. These results in your dog's work can then be assessed by the judge.

One of the instructions given out in obedience clubs regarding footwork is that a handler should step off with his or her left foot when taking the dog forward at heel, and to step off with the right foot when telling the dog to stay.

This seems to be very rigid in Australia, but I only ever heard this from a few instructors in England. While I agree that this can be advantageous when training some dogs, I never make it a hard and fast rule. I always think that when people first start training their dogs they have enough to think about without having to remember on which foot they should step forward.

I step off with either foot, whether I want my dog to heel with me or stay. My dog obeys my voice. Although there is no rule about which foot you should step off with in obedience trials, judges have asked me why I sometimes use my left foot, and sometimes my right. I used to get the impression that they thought I was trying to pull a fast one. But no, I just like to get my dog to obey my voice. If I want him to work by signals, I beckon him with my left hand in a forward movement for him to go with me at heel, and signal with my right hand for him to stay (as described in Chapter 9). I leave this entirely to the individual handler, just as I would with the commands he or she may wish to use. Words of command which appear in the *Obedience Trial Rule Book* are given as examples. These are set out very well and are self explanatory. So where it says 'Drop' you could substitute this with 'Down', 'Flat', 'Lie', or any other word if you wish.

One day I was invited to instruct a group of people at an obedience club. In this group a young lady warned me that she spoke to her dog in Lithuanian. I was quite happy about this, because, after all, dogs respond to sounds and not to actual words. It was amusing in a way when she carried out a recall in front of the whole class. I gave her the orders 'Forward. Halt. Leave your dog. Right-about turn. Halt. Call your dog. Finish. Exercise Finish.' With each instruction I gave, she commanded her dog in Lithuanian and her dog responded perfectly.

I felt I had to take my hat off to this dog. It knew more about a foreign language than I did!

17

Drop on Recall

To be able to drop your dog on a recall or at any time when it is running around can be a very useful exercise. You never know when you might have to use it. There have been numerous occasions where dogs' lives have been saved when unexpected dangers have arisen. But for the quick reactions of their handlers, these dogs could have been killed or seriously injured.

Regrettably, when there have been fatalities many owners have said in retrospect, 'If only I had been able to drop my dog, I could have prevented that terrible accident.' So, first and foremost, we should all aim at teaching our dogs this exercise. After all it is safety first.

If you are an obedience trial enthusiast, you will have to teach your dog how to drop on the recall in the open trial. And to be eligible for this trial, he must qualify as companion dog in the novice trials.

One of the biggest mistakes which handlers make when they reach this stage in the dog's working life is to drop him every time they do a recall. I think they get carried away too much with what is required in the open trial. If you continuously drop your dog on the recall, you are very likely to end up with one of two common faults, and perhaps both.

The first is that because he is expecting to be dropped he will get slower and slower at his recall. This is a great pity, especially when you think of all those months of hard work which you have put in to develop a speedy recall. The second is that he may anticipate the drop and actually drop earlier than the judge orders you to drop him. Therefore it is a bad thing to do too many drops on recall. Instead do about one drop in every ten recalls. If you do it this way, you should always retain a speedy recall. At the same time he should drop instantly on the very few occasions you want him to, and when competing in the open trial.

When you come to train your dog for this exercise, he must have reached the standard in advanced heel work whereby he will drop instantly on your command and signal.

If, like most people, you have found it difficult to teach him to drop when he was walking beside you, you may now think it will be even harder to drop him from a distance. Well, it is not really difficult; in fact, it is quite easy.

121

Take your dog out for a run on your local reserve. When he has been running around for a little while, pick the opportunity when he is going to run towards you, or past you in any direction. Give him the command 'Drop' when he is about 2 or 3 metres from you. As you say this, quickly raise your hand and cast it towards the ground as you go to him. He should obey this instantly, and you will be in an ideal position to uphold your command. Without any hesitation praise him vocally and physically. After a few seconds tell him to 'Go free'. After all, this is really his play time. Let him have another romp around and drop him once again when he is least expecting it. Do not forget to praise him immediately, and always be in a good position — 2 or 3 metres away.

You only need to do this a few times when you take him out for his daily romp. As the days go by, you can try dropping him from a little bit further away each time. Even when you can drop him at a distance of 20 or 30 metres, make sure you run up to him and praise him.

When you are certain that he will obey your command 'Drop' at any time, at any place, and under a variety of circumstances, you can then apply it in the recall exercises.

Carry out a simple recall and when he gets about half way, drop him. As you give him the command and simultaneous hand signal, run towards him. Praise him as soon as you reach him. Running towards him will also have a good effect on him. You will notice that he will go down immediately, and not creep on a little way like some dogs do. When you have praised him tell him to stay and retreat back to your original calling position. Wait a second or two and call him in in the normal way and finish.

When you feel that he has really mastered the exercise, there will be no need for you to go forward every time and praise him. By this time he will be quite happy about dropping as you have praised him and made it an enjoyable part of the exercise.

As far as the obedience trial rules are concerned, you are allowed to use your dog's name 'Rex, come!' when you call him initially, and when you call him from the drop position.

I always say that a good working dog is one which will work anywhere and not just in the ring. So when you go out for a stroll with your dog, put in an occasional drop when he is least expecting it. You should also try getting him to sit, and stand, when he is a few metres away from you. The sit is very important, as you will need this to teach him directional jumping. I shall talk about this in Chapter 21.

18

Stays out of Sight

Before you train or expect your dog to stay while you go out of sight, he must be reliable at staying when you are in sight. When I use the word reliable in this context I mean that he should not mind you leaving him, walking around him, walking in different directions and for varying distances away, stepping over him, and getting him to stay in the midst of distractions.

If you want him to stay for anything up to about three minutes, you can put him in either the sit or down position. However, if it is going to be for any longer, then it is best to put him in the down position, so that he can relax.

When you decide that he is ready for out-of-sight work, it is best to leave him and hide behind something which is only a few metres away—something through which he can partially see you and through which you can watch him. A thinnish hedge, a bushy shrub, a motor car, or shoulder-height wall are ideal for this purpose. Being only a few metres away, you will be in a good position to correct him if he moves.

Many dogs, particularly those who are very attached, become very anxious when they lose sight of their owners. Con-

sequently they break and dash off to find them in the direction they last saw them. I do not regard this as disobedience, but plain anxiety which affects a dog's nervous system.

On the other hand, some dogs break and either run off in another direction, or just wander around to enjoy a good old sniffing session. These dogs have neither anxieties nor respect. Therefore one could regard them as disobedient. The fault lies with the owners. They obviously have not got the respect from their dogs in the first place.

Because this exercise is a new dimension in the dog being trained to stay, it is a good thing for you to keep reappearing. This gives confidence to the dog who may need it, and it impresses upon the clever dog, who possibly has intentions of nicking off, that you are still there keeping a beady eye on him.

I also recommend that you start these out-of-sight exercises by only doing them for very short durations of time, to achieve continued success.

As the days and weeks progress you should be able to hide behind something more and more solid and for longer periods of time. Always make sure that you can see him, even if he cannot see you. The best set-up I have ever seen in an obedience dog club was a screen with very small peep-holes through which handlers could watch their dogs.

When you reach the stage that you know your dog will stay while you are completely out of sight for a few minutes, you can then extend the distance between him and your hiding place. Remember the principle—always be in a position to do something about it. In these early training days of stays out of sight you should not be too far away from your dog. If you are a long way away and he gets up, it will take you time to get back to him and take him back to his original position. You cannot afford to waste this time. All corrections must be made in the shortest possible time.

When doing a stay out of sight and your dog gets up from either the sit or the down, immediately say 'No'. Get to him in haste and replace him in the appropriate position. Tell him 'Stay' and try the exercise again. I hate to see handlers going back to their dogs which have moved and then shouting and getting grossly annoyed with them. Without realising it, they very often upset their dogs by chastising them like this. If they are in a line-up of dogs at an obedience club, they can also upset other people's dogs, especially the sensitive ones.

Handlers shouting their heads off like this will be doing no good to themselves. Anger expressed in this way will be detected immediately by their dogs. Dogs often associate this anger in their handlers with their actual return. Then when the dogs do stay, they move when the handlers return to them at the end of the exercise. In such cases, the dogs move in fear. This is clearly seen in the sit-stay exercise. A dog having had a severe chastisement for moving

during this exercise, drops down as soon as he sees his handler return to him.

So remember, one word 'No' is quite sufficient when a dog gets up. Then take him back and teach him again.

If your dog is at a sit-stay position and he lies down for reasons of boredom or tiredness, do not say 'No' but go back to him and tell him 'Sit up'. You can do this either by standing very close and directly in front of him or by standing beside him. In either case attract him upwards with your voice. When you do this keep your head well above his. This will have an effect of drawing him up towards you. It may also be necessary to snap your fingers in the same direction. This will help him to respond and understand. As he responds give him brief praise, tell him 'Stay', and start again.

If, however, your dog goes down from the sit in order to sniff, say 'No' and go back immediately, take hold of his collar, say 'Sit up' in a firm tone, and give him a jerk up. Tell him 'Stay' and start the exercise again.

So if your dog goes down, it is up to you to read your dog. Quickly work out why he has done it and take the appropriate action. In the first case the dog could have been mentally and physically tired; in the second case he definitely wanted his own way and went straight down to have a good sniff.

If your dog goes down in the sit through lack of interest, there is a method which will help to prevent this.

Sit him on level ground and a few metres back from a descending incline. Tell him 'Stay', walk forwards and go down the incline. As you go he will be able to see less and less of you until he can see only the top of your head as you face him. Very slowly bend down and then up again. Do this a few times. This should keep him interested, and in order for him to watch

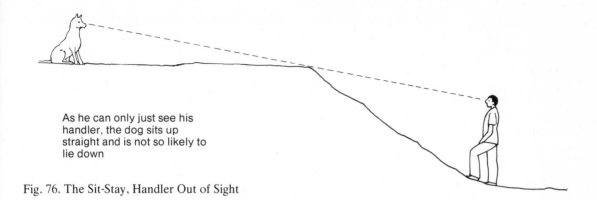

As he can only just see his
handler, the dog sits up
straight and is not so likely to
lie down

Fig. 76. The Sit-Stay, Handler Out of Sight

you he will will have to keep his head up as high as he can (fig. 76).

When you leave your dog and go out of sight, as far as he is concerned you are just around the corner from the point at which you disappeared. You could, of course, walk right around the block and view him from a different direction. You want to try it sometime, and you will see him watching the corner around which he last saw you disappear. However, if you carry out this type of observation, make sure that your scent is not being blown from your viewing point towards him. If this happens, you will see him turn his head in your direction in order to wind scent you. He will scent that you are roughly in that direction even though he may not be able to pin-point your hiding place with his eyes.

Dogs working in open classes of Australian obedience trials are required to do a three-minute sit-stay and a five-minute down-stay, both out of sight. In the utility class, they have to do a ten-minute down-stay out of sight, but no sit-stay.

Many handlers practise these stays in their daily training and time them more or less down to the last second. As I mentioned in Chapter 6, dogs develop a very good sense of time. It is not surprising then to see some dogs get restless when the set time is nearly up. To prevent your dog anticipating the end of the stay exercise you should vary the time of these stays. It is a good idea occasionally to exceed the required times. By doing this you will make sure that your dog can stay there for the full time laid down in the obedience trial rules.

It is an equally good idea occasionally to return to your dog well before this set time is up. By doing this you will surprise your dog and show him that you can return at any time. In other words you will always keep him guessing as to when you will return to him. This will stop him getting ideas that he can mess around when he expects you to be away for a long length of time and well out of range.

Many years ago I was training a particularly clever bitch. I found that she started crawling forward in the down-stay, but only when I left her to walk a long distance away and go out of sight. She did not do this crawling straight away, but usually after about two minutes. Apart from it being difficult to see her crawl slowly from a long distance away, I was not in an ideal position to correct her.

I found a derelict house with upstairs

rooms. Leaving her at the down-stay below an upstairs window, I walked across a large overgrown lawn and then out of sight around the back of some stables. I was then able to run behind other buildings, enter the rear of the house, go up the back stairs, and view her from a window. I had managed to do all this before she had made any move. She was still looking across the lawn to the stables where she had last seen me. I stood silently at the window with the word 'No' on the tip of my tongue. It was not long before she made her first move to crawl. At that instant I let out a sharp 'No'.

She got the surprise of her life! For me to correct her from about 5 metres above her was possibly the last thing in the world she expected.

After using this method a few times in similar situations, her crawling act ceased. If the dog could have talked, I think she would have said, 'I just can't get away with it any more. My master seems to appear from nowhere and his voice instantly corrects me!' Even though dogs cannot talk, this is the impression we should convey to them if we want to gain and maintain their respect for us.

19

How to Speak on Command

Some people regard teaching a dog to speak as a trick, like the trick of getting him to shake hands. For the enthusiastic handler who wishes to compete in the utility classes of obedience trials it is an optional exercise.

For those who train certain types of working dogs it is an essential exercise. The best example of this is found in the highly trained police dog. This is the way he will have to communicate with his handler when he is out of sight, but more about this later.

To speak is quite an easy exercise to teach your dog. There are two main ways of bringing it out in him.

The first is a very natural way. Like the vast majority of dogs your dog will probably bark when someone knocks on your front door. As he barks say 'Speak' several times and, as he responds, praise him 'Good dog'. When you think he has barked enough and you do not want to keep the person outside waiting any longer, give him the command 'Quiet'.

The second way is somewhat natural too. When you feed him hold his bowl of food up and keep saying 'Speak. Speak'. After a while he will become quite agitated and he should come out with a bark, as

much as to say 'Come on, I want my food'. Praise him immediately he barks, then give it to him. He will catch on to this very quickly and later the command 'Speak' will stimulate him to bark even when you have no food.

As soon as he has reached the stage when he will bark on your command you can introduce it as you practise for the trials. Sit him first and then just stand in front of him. Tell him to speak two or three times, and then return and praise him. Then try it with him in the stand position, also in the down position. As training progresses over the weeks gradually move further and further back from him when he is in the down position. In this position he is required to speak when you are at least 4 metres away.

Dogs which compete regularly in the trials get to know the sequence of all the exercises. The keen ones soon get to know what it is all about even before they are told to speak. They recognise the pattern of everything their handlers do.

In British police dog trials the dogs have three exercises where they are required to speak. One is included in the obedience section of the work and the other two in searching for persons in buildings, and property.

The policeman sends his dog into a building where he has to search for a hidden person. That person could be concealed in a cupboard or in a loft. The handler, who remains outside the building, is allowed to control and direct his dog from one place to another until it is obvious that the dog has located the scent of the hidden person. The dog has to indicate clearly that he has made his find by barking. He then has to remain with the hidden person until his handler arrives. A reasonable time is allowed for this exercise, as long as it does not exceed a quarter of an hour.

In the search for property test an irretrievable article is placed in an area out of sight of the dog and his handler. The police dog has to search for the article and indicate its presence by barking. He has to stay by it until his handler arrives. This exercise has to be done within five minutes. The type of article used could be a component part of an engine—something far too heavy for a dog to pick up.

This type of exercise involves two-way communication between man and dog, even though they cannot see each other. The handler commands and encourages his dog to find, and the dog indicates by barking that he has found the person or article.

A dog who barks can be a great asset, provided the barking can be controlled. Most people want a dog who will warn them when someone comes to their house, and one who will warn off would-be intruders. However, a dog who barks incessantly and cannot be stopped is a perfect nuisance to everyone. That is why some people who fear having this trouble when owning a dog play safe and get a Basenji, which cannot bark.

When a dog barks he expresses his state of mind. As you live with your dog, you will hear the different ways in which he barks. In fact, you will learn how to interpret nearly every type. He will express his anger in an aggressive tone, defence in a fearful tone, protectiveness in a warning tone, or eagerness to chase after something in an excited tone. He will give an excitable bark when he goes out for a walk, a joyful bark when you come home, or he could bark in a monotonous tone all day long to express his boredom at being shut up in a pen. Poor old fellow!

It is amazing how instinctively dogs communicate with us in times of trouble. One day when I was indoors my dog raced into the house barking. The tone was most alarming and the barks were rapid. She was obviously trying to attract my attention and kept rushing backwards and forwards to the back door. I followed her and she lead me up the garden to our close-boarded boundary fence. There I heard the German Shepherd dog next door, in distress. I climbed over the fence to find that his kennel chain, which was linked to a run wire, had become entangled with a small tree. I released it and all was well. I later told the owners, who had been out at the time, and they fixed up a pen, which was far better. The German Shepherd's distress cries had been heard by my bitch and, if she had not communicated with me, it could have proved fatal for the dog next door.

20

Food Refusal

The first step you should take in teaching this exercise is to get your dog to sit beside you while you put his bowl of food down on the floor. Here he must learn to stay until you tell him that he can eat it. I believe that every dog should be taught this from puppyhood onwards. If you do this, you will gain much respect from your dog and the chances of him worrying your friends for food when they come to dinner will be lessened.

It is very easy to teach this exercise. Just put your dog on a leash and make him sit. Hold the leash fairly short but not tight in your left hand, and slowly put the food bowl down with your right hand in front of you and slightly to your right, so that it is out of his immediate reach. If he tries to lunge at it, say 'No! Leave', and jerk him up and make him sit again.

When he has remained quite still for a few seconds say 'You can have it', and gesture to him with your hand, sweeping your hand down from his nose towards the food bowl. As he responds praise him vocally 'Good dog'. As the days go by, you can progress through further stages. Put the food further away; extend the waiting time; say other things which he must learn to ignore, and only respond to the appropriate command. Then when you reckon that he is reliable, try doing the exercise off the leash.

The next stage is to get other people to offer him food, firstly by offering it to him with their hands, and then by dropping it on the ground in front of him. As this will be something new to him it is always best to have him on the leash so that you are in a position to correct him with a jerk if necessary. Just before the food is offered to him give the command 'No! Leave'. It is important to get your word in first. He should respect your voice and your presence. When he has refused the food and it has been removed, praise him. After all, he has obeyed your warning and has not attempted to eat it.

Before long you will be able to move further away from him. Furthermore, you will not have to say 'No! Leave' every time, but just 'Stay'. He will soon understand that when food is offered to him by anyone else he must refuse it. Finally, when he has reached the stage of being trustworthy, try it with your back to him. If you happen to have an ultra-clever dog who will only refuse food when you watch him but not when you turn your back on him, then watch him in a mirror. He will get a great surprise when he finds that you can correct him when you are facing the other way, as if you had eyes in the back of your head.

In the utility class, where food refusal is an optional exercise, dogs are offered food on three separate occasions, either consecutively or at different times between exercises. It is conducted in three positions, the sit, stand, and down. The food consists of three different varieties, including cooked or raw meat, cheese, cake, milk, etc. When handlers leave their dogs they have to stand about 5 metres away.

Teaching a dog food refusal for obedience trials does not necessarily guarantee that the dog will never eat from someone else outside the obedience ring. The exercise could therefore be regarded as being somewhat artificial. If handlers were told to go completely out of sight and the judge just casually dropped a piece of meat in front of each dog as he walked by, then it is very probable that some dogs would eat it.

This was the way it was done in the English Obedience Test 'C' many years ago. In my opinion this was a much more natural way of doing it, but, although we trained our dogs to refuse food in the ring, there were always some dogs which would eat food outside the ring environment, whether it was offered to them or not.

Some handlers have been known to train their dogs so well in food refusal that they have disadvantaged themselves when they had to put their dogs into kennels. These dogs would rather go hungry than be fed by their kennel attendants.

When my family and I first arrived in Australia we rented a house for a few months. The owners, who were on holiday abroad, left their Black Labrador called Prince at home. A neighbour came in daily to attend to the dog's needs.

Soon after our arrival we offered to look after Prince and save the neighbour the bother of coming in every day. Now Prince was completely untrained, and, knowing that he was going to be with us for the next six months, I set about training him. He learned all his basic obedience in a very short time. This included sitting for his food every evening. After about four months we bought a home of our own a few kilometres away and felt it only right to take Prince with us until his owners returned.

The day they were due home I took him back so that he would be there to greet them. I left a note to say that he had been no trouble and that I, being a guide dog trainer, had given him some basic training to which he had responded extremely well.

About two days later, his owners telephoned to thank us for all we had done. But what they could not understand was why he did not want to eat. They said that when they put his food down in the middle of the kitchen floor he would just sit there and look at it. This of course was quite out of keeping with him as far as they were concerned, for up until the time they went abroad he used to jump up and nearly knock the bowl out of their hands at feeding time.

On hearing this, I had to smile. I just could not credit that the training I had given him during those few months had been so firmly implanted in his mind. Apologising for my oversight in not telling them that I had taught him to sit for his food, I told them they had to say 'You can have it' and give a hand signal towards the bowl of food. This they did and Prince responded from that time on for evermore.

From time to time in certain areas dogs are poisoned by baits. I always think that people who carry out these dreadful acts must be mentally deranged. Furthermore, they do not stop to think what might happen if small children should pick up these poisoned baits before dogs do.

If you teach your dog food refusal really well, this could prevent him from becoming a victim of a poisoner. However, this training cannot necessarily be regarded as foolproof. No matter how well you have trained your dog, there is always that slim chance that he will eat a bait.

It can be a terribly worrying time for dog owners when they know that a poisoner is on the prowl in their district. My advice in such cases is to keep your dog inside. When you let him outside inspect your garden and ensure that there is no foreign food about. If you leave your dog in an open back yard and you are away from the premises, this is where the poisoner can strike.

I wish that there was a positive answer to this problem, but there does not appear to be one. All we can do is to minimise the risk by taking every necessary precaution we can and hope that the courts will punish severely those who are found guilty of this dreadful crime.

21

Signal Exercise

The giving of visual signals in dog training has two uses. Firstly they assist and help to stimulate response to vocal commands. Secondly they are of great value when commands cannot be given.

In the utility class one exercise is known as the signal exercise. In it the dog is required to work by responding to visual signals only. It demands 100 percent concentration on the dog's part. It also demands great accuracy on the handler's part in order to get prompt responses. While many dogs, particularly those within certain breeds, are very receptive to signals, they can also be confused if the signals are not consistent in their pattern and speed of being given. In the signal exercise your dog has to obey signals to heel, stand, stay, down, sit, come, and finish to heel.

You will often see a handler step forward with his left foot first when commanding to heel, and with his right foot first when commanding his dog to stay. This is carried on through the dog's training, with the vocal commands gradually being dropped. This is quite a good idea, but not all dogs are reliable on this type of signal. I do not make any hard and fast rule about which

foot I step off with. I find it very easy for the dog to respond to a forward hand movement given with my left hand as I say 'Heel' (fig. 77). The command is gradually left out and the dog obeys the hand signal. Signalling the dog to stand and stay is the same as explained in previous chapters (fig. 78). Dropping the dog by signal (fig. 79) is the same as mentioned in Chapter 17 Drop on the Recall.

Now we come to a new movement, and that is to sit the dog up from the down position. Stand about 1·2 metres in front of him. Say 'Sit' and step a little towards him, encouraging him to sit up. As you say 'Sit' signal to him by bringing your right index finger up quickly and just over your head (fig. 80). Praise immediately he responds. When he has become good at this, you will be able to gradually extend your distance and leave off taking paces towards him as you say 'Sit'. The distance you have to be away from your dog in the trial is at least 4·5 metres. From there the next thing you have to do is to signal your dog to come (fig. 81). and then to finish to heel. This is very easy when you come to think of all the times you have recalled him with

Above: Fig. 77. *Hand Signal for the Forward in Heel Work* The command 'Heel' which accompanies this signal is gradually reduced. Eventually the dog will respond to the signal alone. *Left:* Fig. 78. *Hand signal to Stand and Stay*

133

Left: Fig. 79. *Hand Signal to Drop* from the stand position. *Centre:* Fig. 80. *Hand Signal to Sit* from the down position. *Right:* Fig. 81. *Hand Signal to Recall* the dog from the sit position

a simultaneous command and signal.

With a working dog the use of signals is essential; you cannot do without them. I came to realise this even more so when I was training guide dogs. These dogs, when working in harness, received simultaneous commands and hand signals. Towards the end of the training the guide dog is worked on commands alone. The reason for this is to ascertain whether or not she will work well on commands only, because her future blind owner may be carrying a case or basket of some description in his right hand.

The hand signals come in very useful when the guide dog is allocated to her new owner. Although the new owner gives the same words of command, the different voice can be like a foreign language to the dog. However, the person can be shown how to give the hand signals (figs 82 and 83). The dog recognises these and responds accordingly. Within a few weeks the guide dog becomes accustomed to the new voice and the hand signals are dropped. So they are necessary in the dog's initial training, and very helpful during the change-over period from guide dog trainer to guide dog owner.

Signals have a multitude of uses in the training of police dogs. A police dog handler never knows when he may have to work his dog on hand signals during the execution of his duties. He may be in a situation where he does not want his presence to be known. Or he may be in a very dangerous position where it would be unwise for him to give a vocal command to his dog. In such cases visual signals are essential.

Left: Fig. 82. *The Right Turn in Guide Dog Work* The arrival at a down kerb is a signal for the guide dog to stop. His owner stands back and indicates the direction she wishes to go with a hand signal to the dog as she commands him 'Right'. *Right:* Fig. 83. *The Left Turn* The guide dog having stopped, his owner goes up to his head and signals to the dog as she commands him 'Left'

135

22

Seek Back and Scent Discrimination

Scent work is one of the most interesting aspects of dog training. During the second World War dogs were trained to detect people who were buried alive under the debris of the London blitz. They were also used by the Royal Air Force to guard aerodromes and other establishments by patroling in company with a handler, and it was found that they could look after vast areas more efficiently and effectively than scores of human guards could. The Army used dogs for many different types of work, including mine detecting, tracking, carrying, messenger work, and finding casualties. It is interesting to note that of the variety of dogs used for these tasks one breed in particular emerged as best suited, and that was the German Shepherd.

This breed has proved that it can do more different types of work than any other. Apart from his sheep herding ability, which his name implies, he is used universally as a police dog and guide dog for the blind. He has virtually taken over from such working breeds as the Bloodhound and the St Bernard. He excels in avalanche rescue work, and in recent years, along with the Labrador, has been trained to use his nose in detecting drugs and explosives.

Seek Back

The prerequisite for this exercise is that your dog must be able to retrieve. Having trained him to do this, you can go on to teach him to find a small piece of wood or leather. Hold it in your hand for a short time so that it gets your natural scent on it. Before you hide it, show it to him and get him interested in it, but do not let him touch it. Tell him to sit and stay and, keeping his attention, mysteriously hide it behind a piece of furniture on the floor. Return to him and cup your hand over his nose for two or three seconds. This will be long enough for him to take your scent. When you put your hand over his nose, do it very lightly. Do not grip hard; he must be allowed to breathe freely. Then give him the command 'Seek', or 'Find' in a very quiet and drawn out tone. You can also use your hand to beckon him to go forward to the article which is only a couple of metres away but just hidden. As soon as he reaches it and sniffs at it say 'Good dog. Fetch', and give him more praise as he picks it up and brings it to you. The rest of the exercise should be carried out as you would do a retrieve. Hide it once again, but this time in a different place, and repeat the exercise.

The next day hide another piece of wood, but do not indicate quite so much as to where you have hidden it. This will make him use his nose a little more. Praise him the instant he sniffs at it. This will immediately give him confidence in knowing that he has found the article you want him to pick up. If he hesitates in picking it up, encourage him to fetch it and praise him as he returns. Try it once again in a different spot and a little further away if he is really keen.

Within a few days he will know what he has to do by your act of putting your hand lightly over his nose. He will also associate the command 'Seek', or 'Find' with having to go forward and search for an article with your scent on it.

When you feel that he understands the exercise use a different article every time. If you use the same article, he may start looking for something which has *his* scent on it. This will have been transmitted to the article by his saliva. It is also wise to use a different type and shape of article each time, otherwise he may be finding it by using his eyesight and not his nose. Make sure that when you hide your article there is nothing else of yours lying around in that area. I remember a case some years ago in England when a dog could not find his master's article in the ring for some reason or other. He then went and sat next to a chair at the ring side. At first sight it looked as if the dog had gone on strike. However, this was far from the truth, for on the back of the chair was his master's jacket. He could not take it off the chair, so he did the next best thing—he sat beside it!

This example will show you how careful you have to be. At all costs you must prevent confusion coming into your dog's mind. Keep it simple for your dog. Gradually extend the distance you want him to go in order to find your article.

Now start out in the open. Select a piece of cut grass which neither you nor your dog has been on. Sit your dog beside you facing down wind (this means the wind must be blowing away from you in the direction you are facing). Tell him 'Stay' walk forward a few metres, put your article down, and return to him on the same track. Give him the scent off your hand and tell him 'Seek'. As he goes to the spot where you have placed the article, he will scent where you have walked. He will not be able to scent the article until he reaches it, as the wind will be blowing away from him. Praise him as soon as he has found it and call him to you.

Now this is actually a seek forward rather than a seek back, but I find it the best way of going about it. When he gets the idea of it you will only have to say 'Seek', and not even bother about giving him the scent. He will know that he has got to find something of yours.

The next stage is to take him to a new area and, as he walks with you at heel, discreetly drop your article behind you on the track. Continue forward into the wind for several metres, about turn, and sit him. Tell him to 'Seek' and point in the direction of your track. He should have no trouble at all in finding the article. In doing so, he will track over where you have walked.

In the next stage you can drop your article as you walk across the wind. When you have walked about four metres do a right (or left) turn into the wind and after a further six metres about turn and halt. He will now have to seek back a distance of about ten metres with a right-angled turn in it. If he manages this all right, you can make a few more turns over a period of time. Do not rush it; do it gradually. With some dogs you can progress to a point, but no further. You should not worry about this. Just keep him at that stage for as long as it takes until it is firmly established, then attempt the next stage.

When a dog does seek back, he does not necessarily have to use his nose by tracking along the ground; he may wind scent the article. You will never know which way the wind will be blowing when you compete in the utility class. Your dog may do one of the following things: (1) Track along the ground (2) Track part way and then wind scent (3) Wind scent entirely (4) Go over the area and retrieve the article by sight.

From a dog-training point of view, except for the last method, the dog is using his nose correctly according to the conditions. Now although the obedience trial rules state that a dog may use his sight to retrieve the article, in my opinion this is not a seek back. I have seen handlers use the same old article every time to the extent that the dog just looks for that article and that alone. It is not very hard for a dog to sight an article like a leather spectacle case, small wallet, small purse or glove.

People who train their dogs like this are really cheating themselves. They do not stop to think what will happen one day when the dog cannot see it; he will probably soon give up and return empty handed. Therefore, I strongly advise people to train their dogs to use their noses. They should use a different article each time and one which is small enough so that it is not easily seen by the dog.

I always look at this seek back exercise from a very practical point of view. Many years ago, when out for a walk one afternoon in one of our picturesque English forests, I found that I had dropped one of my gloves. There was about 5 cm of snow covering the ground and it was getting dark. In those conditions I knew that I would not stand a chance of finding it. I gave my Border Collie Bob the scent off my hand and told him to seek back. Off he went while I stood there in the bitter cold. After a few minutes he came back with the lost glove in his mouth.

On another occasion I lost a large key to our stables. Although I knew that it must be in a given area, no larger than 2000 square metres, it was like looking for a needle in a haystack. Being autumn, the ground was covered with dead leaves and this made the task almost impossible. I gave Bob the scent and, after quartering the ground for some time, he found it among the leaves. It always gives me a great sense of satisfaction when my dogs can help me by using their own natural ability, because all the hard work I have put in has been brought to fruition.

Scent Discrimination

When your dog can do a simple seek back, scent discrimination is quite easy. Arrange for a friend to put an article down on the ground and then place your own article about half a metre beyond it. Have your dog on the leash, give him your scent, and walk him up to the articles, saying 'Seek'. Allow him to sniff at your friend's article. He should then ignore this and proceed to yours. As soon as he does, praise him and encourage him to pick yours up and bring it to you. Next, try it with a few other articles which have different scents on them and place yours at the end of the line. Allow him to sniff every article and praise him when he comes to yours. The next stage is to put a few more down and, when he comes to yours, see if he will pick it up on his own initiative. Praise him when he does. From then on you should not have any trouble. He will understand that he has to pick up only yours and will associate the scent you have given him with the article which carries the same identical scent.

If however, he picks up the wrong article, just take it away from him. Then immediately show him the correct article and praise him. There are sometimes very logical reasons why a dog picks up the wrong article. It may be that somehow or other the handler has unintentionally touched it, and it does not take much for a minute drop of scent to get on to an article. It may be that the wind is blowing the scent from your article on to another. In this case the dog picks up your scent just as he is over the other article, and he picks it up. It may be that the owner was standing previously on the spot where another article is placed. The dog seeks along the line of articles and smells the scent of his master coming up off the floor around the article and naturally picks that article up. These are just some of the things which can confuse the dog. So you need to check and double check everything when you train your dog in scent work.

In the utility class the handler may provide a group of articles which consists of three sets each comprising of five identical articles, one set each of wood, leather, and metal. The articles are numbered and the handler chooses one from each set and the remaining twelve articles are placed at random in a ring. Now if the dog finds the three designated articles, he could be seeking articles which have the strongest scent on them. However, he may pick up any of the other articles because the handler's scent could be on every one of them. Even if they have all been washed and put in a box and conveyed in the handler's car, they could still hold faint traces of his scent. As far as a dog is concerned, a handler's scent in his car can contaminate anything conveyed in it. So to safeguard anything going wrong in this scent discrimination exercise it would be best for someone else to provide the articles and not the handler.

Years ago in England I was competing in Test 'B' Obedience with a Border Collie. In the scent discrimination exercise the dog has to find the handler's scent on an article provided by the judge. Up to nine other similar articles are put down. The articles on that occasion were pieces of carpet 5 cm square. With my dog facing away from the articles, I placed my own, which I had held in my hand, on the steward's programme sheet. Holding it down on the sheet with the aid of his pencil the steward placed it among the other nine articles, stood back a few metres, asked me to about turn and send my bitch in to find it. I gave Lassie my scent and the command 'Seek'. Off she went, but instead of going to the articles she went up to the steward and sniffed the centre of his programme which he was holding down at his side. She was just about to take it out of his hand, but paused for a moment. Then, seeing the articles a few metres away, she went straight over to them, found mine very quickly, brought it in, and was awarded full marks. If she had taken the steward's programme, which would have been hilarious, I would have been just as pleased, because she was using her nose correctly. This shows how quickly human scent can be transferred from one article to another —in this case it took only a few seconds. The steward and I both learned something from that episode. He was made aware of how he should conduct himself so that nothing like that should happen again. We never stop learning, do we!

Many years ago, when I first started training, the practise of giving a dog a scent was grossly overdone. So much so that it made it difficult for some dogs to find the right article, while other dogs failed completely.

In those days we used to hold the dog's head still with our left hand and put our right hand fairly tightly over his nose for him to take in our scent. We also put our ear close to his nose to listen to him taking in at least three deep and strained breaths. Having done this, we were sure, so we thought, that he really had the scent. Well yes, he really did have it. He had far too much of it, in fact. When he went up to the articles all he could smell was his master's scent. Little wonder that he was confused! Many dogs just picked up the first article they came to, others wandered around confused, while the rest found the correct articles. Many of the dogs which had received too much scent used to give a big sneeze before they reached the articles. At the time most handlers did not realise why they did this, but I think that it was the dogs' way of clearing their nasal systems of a large amount of the scent they had been given. This gave them a much better chance to discriminate and find the correct articles.

Another method of giving scent was to place one hand over the dog's nose and gently massage his chest with the other. Perhaps handlers thought they were assisting their dog's lungs to draw in more scent through their noses. To anyone who did not know, this looked as if the dog was receiving some form of artificial respiration! Even in dog training it is essential to have a sense of humour and, if you ever wanted to be amused, this was a sight not to be missed.

Then one day some dog-training enthusiast came up with a very logical theory as to why so many dogs were failing in scent discrimination. He believed that dogs were being given too much scent by their handlers. He said that if any of us sniffed at a bottle of strongly scented perfume for long enough we would not be able to smell any other scent for the next few minutes, because we would be overburdened with the one we had just inhaled. On the other hand, if we took only a minute sniff of that scent, we would be able to discriminate among different perfumes and find the right one. As the idea got around, handlers changed their techniques and let their dogs have only a brief sniff when they gave them the scent. Those who did this found that the comical artificial respiration had no effect at all, and the dogs trotted out to the articles without having any more fits of sneezing.

When your dog can do a seek back, seek forward, and scent discrimination really well, you could then try him out on a stranger's scent to find the stranger's article. This exercise is not included in Australian obedience trials, but you will find it in Test 'C' of the English obedience tests.

A piece of marked cloth having the judge's scent on it is placed in the ring by a steward. The handler receives a similar piece of cloth from the judge from which the dog takes the scent. These pieces of cloth are approximately 15 centimetres square, and not more than 25 centimetres square. The number of cloths among which the dog has to discriminate does not exceed ten. One or more of these are decoy scents, i.e., cloths with different human scents on them.

Apart from this being an obedience exercise in competitive work, it can have its practical use. You never can tell when you may need it. If a friend of yours loses something in a given area, your dog could be given the person's scent and he could very well be successful in finding the lost article.

When you come to teach your dog on a stranger's scent, it is a good idea to do it with a friend, someone whom your dog knows fairly well. Start off by doing it in the form of a simple seek forward. If this is successful, the next day a fresh article which has been held by your friend should be put down, plus an article which belongs to someone else, preferably someone whom the dog does not know. Now give your dog the scent of your friend by means of a separate piece of cloth. As he discriminates between the two, praise him when he comes to your friend's article. When this proves to be successful you can start increasing the number of articles. Because it is something new, you need to start from the beginning again by using your voice to reassure the dog that he is doing the right thing. Remember to keep it simple. When he can find things belonging to your friend try him with someone else he knows, but not on the same day. Have a good gap between each lesson and use many different people to provide the decoy articles. Avoid using your friend (the ones for whom the dog has found articles) to provide the decoys. It all needs much thought and care, until in the end you start thinking like a dog! This is good when you can do this, because you will be less likely to make mistakes which can confuse your dog.

As I said before, scent work is a fascinating subject and one with which you can have a lot of fun. In the early 1950s, when obedience training was getting underway, handlers from the very few dog training clubs used to get together and put on demonstrations at carnivals and fêtes.

On one such memorable occasion the late Mrs Gil Hester had a great idea. She said, 'We'll show our audience that the dogs can read their own names!' There were about eight of us in the demonstration team, and she wrote our respective dogs' names on pieces of card. These were rolled up individually and held tight with rubber bands. We kept them in our possession for a few days before the day of the carnival. The demonstration was a great success and we were ably assisted by an excellent commentator on the microphone. Our show was brought to a climax when he announced that the dogs would show everyone that they could read their names. As he said this our scrolls, together with several blank ones, were placed in the ring. We discreetly gave our dogs our scents, and they went in two by two and returned a scroll to each handler. Each dog's name was announced before the scroll was unrolled and shown to the audience. The huge crowd of people were amazed and gave great applause. Our humorous commentator, feeling that the people should be let into the secret, went on to explain that each dog's name was printed in smaller letters on the outside of the scroll. All the dog had to do was to read each one until he found his own!

We put on a similar demonstration to prove that our dogs were not colour blind. Each one of us had a piece of rod painted a bright colour, and we all had pieces of broad ribbon of corresponding colours, which we showed our dogs and tied on to their collars. It looked very spectacular to see each dog go into the centre of the ring and pick up a rod bearing the same colour as his ribbon.

This shows how obedience can be great fun and very entertaining for the general public.

23

Directional Jumping

This is a very complex exercise and although it is included in our utility class, in my opinion it has no practical everyday use. However, it does test the dog's initiative and obedience. It also tests the handler's control over his dog at a distance where he has to use hand signals as well as his voice.

The two jumps (the high jump and the bar jump) are placed midway in the ring and approximately 7·5 metres apart. The handler, with his dog standing at heel, takes up a midway position about 6 metres from the jumps. The judge orders the handler to send his dog between the jumps towards the opposite side of the ring. When the dog is approximately 6 metres past the jumps, the handler has to tell his dog to sit. The handler is allowed to attract the dog's attention by using his name when commanding him to sit. Although the dog is not required to sit square on to the handler at this point, in training I always ensure that he does. My reason for this is that if a dog is sitting at an angle facing one of the jumps he is likely to go over the jump he is looking at, even though you may command and signal him to jump the other one.

When the dog has sat, the judge indicates to the handler which jump he wants the dog to take first. The handler commands and signals the dog to clear the jump indicated. The handler may give a command to jump at each jump, but the word used must be different to the word used to call the dog. While the dog is jumping, the handler may turn and face the dog so that it will come in to him squarely. On order from the judge the handler commands his dog to finish. Praise is permitted at this stage. The same procedure follows for the dog to go over the remaining jump.

You may think that it is going to be an extremely hard task, if not an impossible one, to get your dog to do all that, but really it is quite easy.

Like everything else in dog training, you have to build as you go. Let us just take a look at all the things the dog is required to do in this complex exercise. He has to heel off the leash, stand, be sent away, turn about, sit, do a recall as directed over one of the two jumps, sit squarely in front, and finish; then he has to do it all over again over the other jump.

Before you attempt this exercise you need to be able to sit your dog at any time, anywhere, and at any distance. This is quite simple if your follow the procedure given in Chapter 16 for getting a dog to drop anywhere before you start the drop on a recall. So when you are out for a stroll with your dog pick the opportunity when he is a few metres from you and tell him to sit. Ensure that he does and praise him. As time goes on, gradually extend the distance between him and you, and immediately he responds to your command 'Sit' go to him and praise him. Then either go forward with him at heel or command him to go free again.

The only other thing you have got to do now is to train him to away from you in a straight line between two obstacles. You have got to make it as easy as possible for him to understand, so set up your high jump and bar jump about 7·5 metres apart, but reduce their heights to about half that which he will be required to jump in competition. You can raise them much later. For the time being keep it simple.

The next thing is to send him from A to B (fig. 84). Now for the time being you need to have your point A between or just beyond the jumps, and not six metres back from the jumps at the recognised sending position. I will explain why later. You have then got to think about giving him an incentive to which he can respond. There are several ways you can do this. First of all leave him in the standing position, walk straight up to point B, and mysteriously put down some article, like your coat, which is not regarded by him as a retrieve article. You must not put down his dumbbell or anything like it. As you put it down, watch him and ensure that his attention is focused on what you are doing. Return to him on the same track and stand beside him. Do not go around the back of him as you return to him as he may cast his head

around to look at you, and this, in turn, may break his concentration on your coat at point B. Without any further ado give him an enthusiastic command 'Away', with a simultaneous signal with your right hand in the direction of your coat. You can also step forward with your right foot, which will enable you to keep your signalling hand down at his eye level. If he is lively and interested in what you have put down, he should run up to it to investigate. As he leaves you quietly follow him, and just before he reaches your coat call out his name. Immediately he turns round say 'Sit' and, without stopping, continue towards him and praise him vocally and physically. You can now see that at this point B he has had two incentives, (1) your coat and (2) your praise.

The next part of the exercise is to call him over the jump. Tell him 'Stay' and position yourself, let's say, behind the high jump which is on the right as your face your dog. Put your right arm over the jump and call him enthusiastically 'Over'. As you say the word lift your right arm up high and to the right, so that he fully understands what you want. Just as he is about to leap over the jump say with great gusto 'Up!'. Instantly praise him as he is in mid-air, and run backwards to the point from which you will be sending him eventually (point C). Praise him again when he comes to sit in front of you and then finish him to heel.

Having got him to go over the high jump, you must now get him to jump over the bar jump. Take him up and stand him at the same point, in between and just beyond the jumps. Leave him and go and re-arrange your coat. Return to him, send him, and praise just as you did before. Tell him to stay, and go behind the bar jump which is on the left. Carry out the same procedure

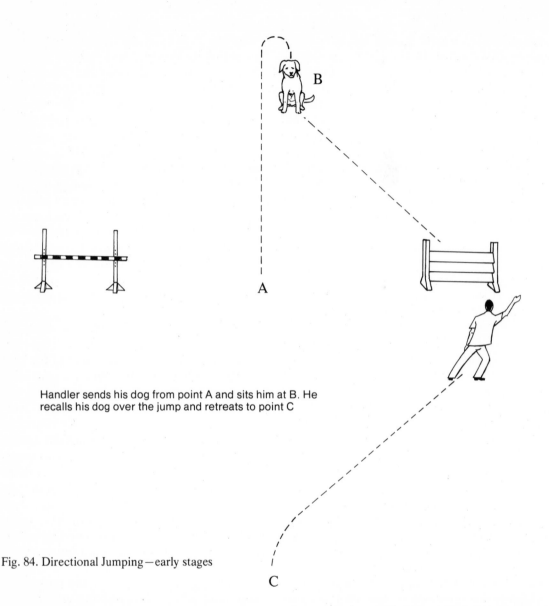

Handler sends his dog from point A and sits him at B. He recalls his dog over the jump and retreats to point C

Fig. 84. Directional Jumping—early stages

as before, only this time you must signal with your left hand.

The matter of how many times you should practise this in your daily training depends largely on your dog, but as a general guide I think twice over each jump is enough. Avoid always having the high jump on the right-hand side and the bar jump on the left. Also do not fall into a pattern of getting him to jump one type first and then the other. Alternate the jumps in this respect as much as you can.

My reason for sending a dog away from a point beyond the jump is so that he can concentrate entirely on point B, where he has to go. The jumps will be out of his mind. If you were to start by sending him from point C (6 metres from the jumps), he may not go straight to the coat (which is about 12 metres away) as he may be confused and go over one of the jumps. This you must avoid at all costs. So as you progress with his training over the weeks, gradually send him from a point further and further back until you can do the full distance. As you progress, he will get to know what he has to do—a send-away first, followed by a recall over one of the jumps. It will soon form a pattern in his mind. In fact, there will be two patterns and the hand signal you give (right or left) will determine which jump he has to take.

Your position behind each jump is very important. To begin with, your dog will go over the jump mainly because you are standing behind it. The appropriate hand which you signal with, will be of great significance to your dog as he progresses through the stages of this exercise. As the training continues, you should gradually modify your position. In the next stage, therefore, instead of standing directly behind the jump, position yourself a little to one side, so that your arm, which gives him the signal, is behind the jump. Your arm signal will then start to take the place of your body. As the weeks of training go by, you can gradually modify your position by standing further back from the jumps and also by positioning yourself nearer and nearer to the centre line along which your dog will be doing his complete send-away.

Your starting position at point A should also be modified. You should gradually stand further and further back until you direct the entire operation from one position (fig. 85). You can gradually phase out the use of your coat, or whatever it was that you put down, by just pretending to put something down each time. When you do this, crouch down very slowly and rub your hand on the ground. Watch him as you do this and you will see his curiosity aroused.

The praise which you give him at point B should be kept up for some time, and then be very gradually phased out. Finally, after many weeks of training, you should be able to conduct the entire exercise over both the jumps from one position. When you can do this, your dog will be ready for that trial.

Now a few words about the dog coming to sit squarely in front of you. The rules state that while the dog is jumping, the handler may turn and face the dog so that he will come into the handler squarely. This I think is a very considerate rule, and the rest is up to the handler to decide at what angle he should face in order to get the best result. Much depends upon how fast the dog goes over the jump, how soon he applies the brakes, and how well he knows the straight position he should adopt every time he comes in to sit in front of the handler. Personally, I like to face point B all the time. This means that when my dog clears the jump he has to come into me on a slight S bend so that he sits with his back towards point B. This is very easy to teach the dog if you follow the procedures of correcting dogs which come in too far over to the left or right in the recall (Chapter 11).

Dogs which excel themselves in directional jumping are those which have a fairly high degree of initiative. Very obedient dogs, such as those who would never think about pulling on the leash, are not always so good—they lack initiative.

At an advanced dog training course I held in Victoria a German Shepherd dog

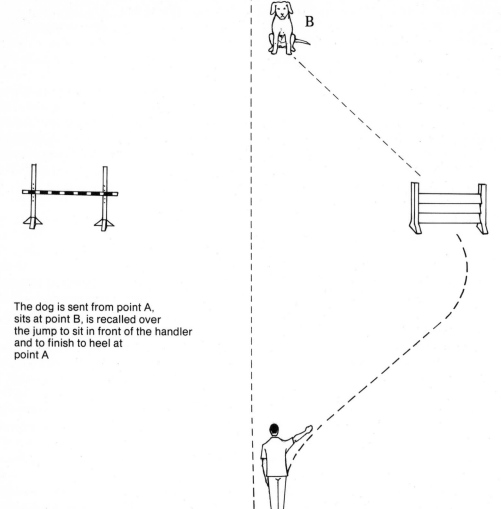

The dog is sent from point A,
sits at point B, is recalled over
the jump to sit in front of the handler
and to finish to heel at
point A

Fig. 85. Directional Jumping—final stage

A

named Lisa had a tendency to lead out too much in heel work. She had to be corrected time and time again, whereas all the other dogs of various breeds knew their heel work extremely well. When it came to learning the send-away in the directional jumping Lisa left the others literally stand-ing. She went straight out because she had that initiative in the first place. After a while a few of the others caught on to the idea, but the rest were lifeless—initiative in them was totally lacking. I believe that one of the reasons for this was probably that these dogs had had far too much heel work drilled into them, so that whatever initiative they may have had in the first place had been destroyed.

I think this is a very important point and one which all handlers should be aware of. They should give their dogs enough obedience training to gain control, but not enough to destroy initiative. One has to get the correct balance in order to have a first-rate working dog.

For those people who want to train their dogs for the send-away, drop, and recall, as required in the English obedience regulations, the same method of sending the dog away can be used as I have described for that required in directional jumping. The differences are that the dog has to be sent from the sitting position and not from the stand, at the end of the send-away he has to drop and not sit, and he completes the exercise by doing a recall to heel instead of going over the jumps.

If you decide to train your dog to do this exercise with the aim of working in tests 'B' and 'C' you need to train for two main conditions. Firstly, some of the tests are held inside large halls where, in order to make the send-away a good distance, the dog is usually required to go right up to the far wall and then drop on command. Secondly, when the tests are held at outside venues, where the dog is still required to be sent away to an appreciable distance, he has no fixed wall to go to, but sometimes open space.

Training your dog in a hall to go away in a straight line to a point on a far wall, or diagonally across the floor to a corner, is comparatively easy. The walls help to a certain extent to guide your dog straight. However, they can also make a dog go slow as he knows that he must slow up as he reaches the wall, otherwise he will end up with a very sore head. Start off by training him to go just a few metres to the wall or to something you have put against it, and drop him. As he drops get to him as quickly as possible to praise him. Tell him 'Stay' and walk away down the hall. When you have gone a few metres call him enthusiastically 'Rex, heel'. Turn your head around to your left side as you say this, which will encourage him to run and join you at heel. You should continue forward with him, possibly putting in a few turns on the way; then halt and praise him again.

To increase the send-away distance in subsequent lessons start him off from a point a little further away from the wall each time, until eventually you should be able to send your dog the full length of the hall.

When you train your dog out in the open you can use the same method, viz., putting something down as a first incentive. When you have sent him away, dropped, and praised him, you want to take the opportunity of walking further on in a continuous straight line, and then call him to heel. You can continue forward with him without doing any turns and finally halt and praise him. Doing it this way during these initial stages you are using the principle of the straight line concept again. If you examine this carefully, you will see that there are three incentives for your dog which are all on the same straight line: firstly he had your coat to go to; secondly he received your praise as he was lying down; thirdly he was recalled to heel as you continued forward to halt finally with more praise.

Apart from training in an open area like a football ground, you could also practise this exercise on a footpath, providing it is in a safe area where there is no traffic. A long straight stretch of footpath, preferably one which has a continuous fence running alongside it, is ideal. The alignment of the fence and the kerb will be a help to you in training your dog to do a straight send-away.

This method can of course be used occasionally in establishing the send-away part of the directional jumping exercise. The only substitution you need to make is that you send your dog from the standing position and you tell him to sit instead of drop.

Finally, I would like to say that, although in the Australian obedience trials we always recall our dogs to sit in front of us before going to heel, it is a good idea for us also to be able to recall our dogs directly to heel whether we are standing still at the time, walking, or even running. Apart from this being a slight variation in recalling the dog, he learns by responding correctly to the command given, viz., that 'Come' means he has to sit in front of you, and 'Heel' means he has to join you at your left side and keep going with you until you halt, when he should sit automatically.

24
The Guard Dog

Let me say first and foremost that the training of dogs to attack, which is known as man-work, should be strictly confined to training establishments which are under Government control. Such places, like those found in the police forces and armed services, have their own trainers and handlers who are experts in this particular field of dog training. The dogs which are used and the men who handle them are specially selected and highly trained. Dogs or handlers who do not measure up to the standards required are not used in this specialised work.

Although I was a qualified instructor at the Royal Air Force Police Dog Training Centre years ago, I would never train civilians and their dogs in attack work. I knew that most owners would not have had the control required, while others might have abused it by threatening people with their 'amateur' police dogs. I would certainly have had no control over their use, and the owners could easily have ended up in court.

In England years ago a young man in our dog club was doing exceptionally well in obedience with his male German Shepherd dog who was a very friendly dog and always willing to work. Then one day an older man, who claimed that he was a very experienced dog trainer, influenced the young man to bring the dog to him so that he could teach him how to attack. The old saying 'a little knowledge is a dangerous thing' could certainly have been applied to that episode. Before long the dog got out of control and was challenging everyone. Eventually he bit someone very badly. The young man was taken to court, and the dog had to be destroyed. I learned later that this upset the young man so much that he ceased to show any more interest in obedience dog training.

Here in Australia, nearly every week I receive telephone calls from dog owners who ask me if I will train their dogs to attack. It seems, that in this modern age when there is so much crime and violence, many people want extra protection. On questioning these people I find, more often than not, that they cannot even be bothered to take their dogs out for walks, let alone being willing to teach them basic training. There are others who, having taught their dogs obedience training, want to go on to

149

man-work, as if it were some sort of post-graduate work. I always refuse to teach man-work and do my utmost to persuade people not to indulge in this dangerous practice.

Unfortunately there are certain people who profess to be experts in this field and set themselves up in business to train dogs in man-work. In doing this they either train the owner with the dog or take the dog in for several weeks, boarding and training it for the owner. The results are, more often than not, disastrous. The trainer does not know what he is doing and the owner knows even less. Because of the bad treatment and harsh training they often receive, formerly good-tempered dogs become wild and aggressive or nervous and aggressive. Usually control over these dogs becomes less and less until it is non-existent. The dog is unreliable and then becomes a complete liability.

What people really need is to have a dog who is well trained in obedience and who will bark and cease barking on command when a stranger approaches their home. The presence of a dog barking in a home to warn approachers that he is there has a psychological effect on any potential house-breaker or burglar. People usually also want a dog who will remain quiet in their car, and not bark continuously and frantically as people walk past it. The sight of a dog in a car will usually deter any car thief, because he will have no idea what the dog might do to him if he tries to get in, and there are usually plenty of other cars about without dogs in them for the would-be burglar to turn his attention to.

Likewise, the sight of a trained dog, walking at heel beside his master or mistress, is a deterrent to anyone who may be contemplating attacking the owner. A dog does not necessarily have to be trained to defend his owner in a dangerous situation — he will do it instinctively, even if he has not shown signs of it before.

So my advice to you is to leave man-work alone; leave it to the Government-controlled organisations. I also advise people not to send their dogs away to be trained. They will have no idea how their dogs are being treated, or how much training they receive. When owners collect their dogs from these places they are usually given a short demonstration of what the dog has been taught, but no instruction as to how they should continue with it.

I have had some clients who have fallen for this and their dogs have come back nervous wrecks. In some cases the trainer has told them that, although many hours were spent on their dogs, they proved very difficult. Because of this the dogs had learned very little. Despite this the trainer charged exorbitant fees for the time he claimed he had put in on the dogs. The owners had no way of knowing how much or how little time he had given the dogs. This type of business is often an unscrupulous racket.

The best and most sure way of having a well-trained dog is for the owner to be trained with his or her dog. Owners can either receive instruction at an obedience dog club or seek private individual training from professional trainers. The latter is usually the best way, especially if the owners have specific problems with their dogs, or if they feel happier being taught alone instead of working in a large class at a dog club.

25

How has the Dog Learned

A dog learns by instinct and by training. Instinct is natural in the dog and training is artificial. It could also be said that instinct is the property of the dog while training is the education the dog receives from his master.

A simple definition of instinct is that it is the inborn memory passed down from one generation to the next within a species. All dogs have some instincts in common, and, as well as this, different breeds possess instincts peculiar to them. Hounds have the hunting instinct, sheepdogs have the herding instinct, and various types of gundog breeds have the retrieving instinct, and so on. When you put dogs of particular breeds to the corresponding types of work, you are combining instinct with training. The dog naturally knows what to do in his own mind; it is just a case of your controlling him with training. This eventually results in man and dog working as a team.

It is not difficult to combine the instinctive actions done by your dog with words you give him. For example, when you see that your dog is going to lie down of his own accord, say 'Down'; after weeks and months of this you will often find that he will lie down whenever you say it. Another common action the dog will do when he stands up after having had a sleep is to stretch his front legs by bowing his head, and then stretch his back legs by leaning forward with his head erect. If you say 'Bow' every time he is about to stretch his front legs, after much training he will make this polite and gracious bow any time you say 'Bow'!

When your dog comes out of water, or when you have given him his daily groom, he will naturally shake his coat. At the instant he starts to shake, or when you reckon he is about to, say 'Shake yourself'. Once again, with much practice over a fairly long period of time, he will shake himself on your command. With all these actions, and any more you would like to have a go with, do not forget to praise him upon his response.

A question often asked is, can a dog learn from another dog? The answer to this is, yes he can, if it is an instinctive action the other dog does which you want your dog to copy. Very often another dog can teach your dog far better than you can yourself. I once had a bitch who would never go in the sea or any water. No matter how much our family tried to encourage her in, even by swimming a fair way out ourselves, she would not venture one step into the sea. Some time later she became very attached to a Labrador bitch named Zeta, who was staying with us. Zeta adored the water and loved swimming out into the sea to retrieve things. Gradually our Border Collie, feeling torn apart from this Labrador, ventured further and further into the water to be with her. Eventually she overcame her fear of the waves and took to swimming.

I regarded this as a great achievement on the part of both dogs, as some dogs are just as likely to learn wrong or bad things from other dogs. One of the most dreaded things in this country is sheep worrying. It only needs a few dogs to go around in a pack in a country area, and before you know it they are chasing and killing sheep. It should be the personal responsibility of every owner to ensure that his or her dog does not stray at any time.

Some young dogs which live in company with nervous dogs can develop the same trait. A client once brought me her four-month-old Chihuahua. The dog had a nervous disposition and it was some time before he would accept me. The lady told me that his mother was very nervous, but his father was as bold as brass! She had been walking and kennelling this puppy with his mother up until then. I advised her to keep the puppy right away from his mother from that time on, and to put him with the sire. Within a week the puppy changed tremendously. He continued to improve every week and before long he was winning in the show ring and soon became an Australian champion. Had the owner not separated him, he would have continued to copy all the nervous actions

and barks his mother made. If this had gone on long enough the fault would have become incurable.

A large number of exercises you teach your dog are based on the theory of the conditioned reflex developed by the Russian physiologist, Ivan Pavlov. He noticed that when food was brought to a dog it began to salivate, and that even before the food entered the dog's mouth the smell of the food and the sight of it coming stimulated the dog's salivary glands to function. Pavlov found that the same effect was produced by other things as well, such as the presence of the people who brought the food, the sound of their voices or footsteps, and the sight or noise of the dishes in which the food was given. He also found that if a bell was rung when the food was given, in due course the dog would salivate on hearing the bell even if no food was present. This reaction of the dog became known as a 'conditioned reflex' produced by a 'secondary stimulus'.

In this context let us examine once again the sit. With much training it becomes for your dog an automatic reflex action activated by different stimuli. Surprisingly enough there are at least eleven of these:

1. The command 'Sit'
2. A jerk up on the leash
3. A forward and downward push on the dog's hindquarters
4. The handler coming to a halt
5. Place, e.g., arrival at a kerb
6. Situation, e.g., the dog doing a recall, retrieve, etc.
7. The sound of the handler's footsteps ceasing
8. The presence of food
9. A hand signal
10. Time
11. Stubbornness

The first four are used in your dog's initial training. When the dog responds to the command 'Sit', the jerk on the leash and push on the dog's hindquarters can be left out. Later the command to sit is gradually dropped and you finally get to the stage where the dog will sit automatically when you halt.

If you make it a practise to sit him at every kerb you come to, he will eventually sit as he arrives at the kerb, even if you are walking behind him, (this is assuming he is walking free in a quiet safe area).

When you reach a certain stage in training he will understand the situation of the recall and sit automatically in front of you. Later, he will understand that he has to do the same in similar situations like the retrieve and the scent discrimination exercises, as well as in the different jumping exercises.

A very well-trained dog will sit not only when he sees you halt, but when he hears your footsteps cease. This can be seen when a handler, who is walking his dog at heel on a pavement, allows it to look directly to the left, at say a stray dog on the other side of the road, and, as he halts, his dog will sit. The dog has not seen his master stop, but he has heard his footsteps cease. But to see this accurate response, you need a highly trained dog.

Teaching a dog to sit for food is very easy, and it is a very good thing to get your dog to sit for his meal and then tell him that he can have it. Within a very short time you will not have to tell him to sit for it, he will do it automatically when he smells, hears, or sees you prepare his dinner.

When you reach the more advanced stages in training your dog you can teach him to sit in response to your hand signal. Your hand signal must accompany your command 'Sit'. If you gradually reduce your command he will eventually respond to just your hand signal.

Some dogs can either be taught, or will sit naturally at a certain place and at a certain time of the day. Dogs have, as I have said before, an incredible sense of time, and provided the daily circumstances surrounding a dog are consistent, he will respond consistently. In my youth, we owned a Border Collie called Bob. He got to know that I would arrive home from school at 4.30 p.m. Like most dogs he selected a place in the garden (in the middle of one of the flower beds) from which he could see me enter our property by the rear entrance. After a while he had worn quite a patch among the flowers where he sat. He took up this position every weekday afternoon. It was his sense of time which stimulated him to do this.

On very rare occasions, clients have brought me very stubborn dogs. They have been the kind which refuse to go for a walk on the leash. After the usual gentle persuasion and encouragement has failed to get such dogs moving, firmer methods have to be used. The command 'Heel' has to be upheld with either a jerk or gradual pull forward on the leash. The dog, who is in the standing position, finds it difficult to resist and will sit. In doing so, he places more of his body weight closer to the ground, which helps to increase his resistance against being pulled forward. In this case it is his sense of balance which controls his body to do this. Dog owners who have this type of problem often admit that they have given in to their dogs' acts of stubbornness. This can be overcome by taking the dog for a walk in a large circular route of about 3 kilometres without stopping. It is a battle of the wills, but after a while the dog will give in and walk. Praise must be given (no matter how worn out the handler is), as soon as the dog responds and for the rest of the walk.

From time to time you will see some dogs sit or respond in other ways to the commands of a class instructor. This usually happens when these dogs have been attending classes every week for a number of months. The dogs hear the instruction (like 'Forward') a fraction of a second before their handlers say 'Heel'. Later the dogs anticipate the command 'Heel' being given and start to move off on the word from the instructor. One way of overcoming this anticipation is for the instructor to tell the handlers to stand still when he says 'Forward' and for them to keep moving when he says 'Halt'. He will only need to do this now and then and, provided the handlers correct their dogs if they happen to respond to the instructor, they will cease to be stimulated by him. Instructors should watch this point very closely.

Another method, which a guide dog instructor uses when training a blind person with his guide dog, is to spell out the word which he wants him to use on the dog, like L E F T for 'left'. It would not be good for the instructor to say the word, otherwise the guide dog would respond to his voice and not to that of her new master. However, if this method is used for long enough, some very clever guide dogs will respond to a word which is spelt out! I remember one of my colleagues spelling out the word S I T to one of his blind pupils, and before she could say 'Sit' to her guide dog, it had sat. This was witnessed by two ladies on the pavement. One turned to the other and said, 'Isn't it marvellous to see what those guide dogs can learn these days. They can even spell!'

A formed conditioned reflex does not always remain permanent. It can be in-hibited. This means that it can be completely broken down or modified. It can be affected by an interfering outside force; this is known as 'external inhibition'. Or it can be influenced by the handler in some way; this is known as 'internal inhibition'.

External Inhibition

Your dog may be working satisfactorily, but is then distracted by a passing dog or cat. If you do not take steps to prevent this distraction, your dog's work will deteriorate. It is therefore necessary for you to concentrate very hard on your dog when training him and do everything to keep his attention on his work. If you do this, all outside distractions will be pushed far into the background of your dog's mind, and he will work perfectly.

Internal Inhibition

This is where your dog's work can deteriorate if you are inconsistent and do not bother to uphold your commands. Imagine that you have trained your dog to sit at every kerb he comes to, until it has become a conditioned reflex. Then you decide to take him straight over kerbs. Within a short time he will cease to sit at any kerb. You will have then inhibited his training in kerb drill. You could classify that as a complete breakdown, and it is something which you certainly do not want to happen. However, some modifications are very acceptable. You will find a good example of one of these in the correction of the crooked sit (Chapter 9). In the early stages of this corrective exercise the dog learns to come to heel in the pattern of a letter S in reverse. Later the dog will do a short cut and shuffle in sideways to you, and this modification is just what you want him to do.

Dogs learn by association of ideas. This means that a dog recognises things and situations which are identical or similar to the ones he has been trained on before. A very good example of this is seen in the training of a guide dog who is taught to stop at all kerbs, find pedestrian crossings, telephone booths, particular shops, etc. The dog can then be taken hundreds of kilometres away to work in another town, and will find similar things and places. The dog will recognise so much by sight and a great deal by scent. Shops, regardless of the thousands of different articles they sell, have common smells within the lines of business they contain. Therefore it is not too hard for a guide dog to find any chemist's shop on the command 'Find the chemist', or any post office on the command 'Find the post office', and so on.

Dogs also learn by means of trial and error. They learn that to go one way will result in an unpleasant sensation, but if they go another way it will be a pleasant sensation. A good example of this is seen in the use of the long check-cord in the recall (Chapter 11).

The process whereby your dog learns by repetition is known as habituation. It is a major factor in your dog's development; every time you take your dog out for a walk or a training session, his training is being renewed, improved, and more and more firmly implanted in his mind to the point where he will never forget it. About the only thing which will prevent him carrying out his work is physical disability.

In the latter stages of training it is a good idea to reinforce all the exercises your dog knows. It is just a case of getting him to obey under the influence of a conflicting force. When you have given your dog a lot of training and you feel that he really knows the sit-stay exercise with his leash on, leave him and stand in front of him. Then say 'Stay' once again, pull very gently on the leash, and then relax it. Try this two or three times, but give him the command 'Stay' as you pull the leash. These slight pulls will be a temptation for him to move, but he must resist them and obey the command to stay. All exercises can and should be reinforced as this will help in making your dog even more reliable.

There has always been some controversy as to whether or not a dog has the ability to reason. My opinion about this has altered over the years, and I now feel that he has his own way of reasoning. It certainly is not the same as any human power of reasoning, and I believe this is because he uses his senses in an entirely different way to the way in which we do. For example, his memory of people mainly relies on three of his senses: sight, hearing, and smell, depending upon the length of time which has elapsed since he last met the person.

During the many years I worked with guide dogs, I was in an ideal position to see their memories at work. Guide dog instructors train their dogs in approximately four months. In that time each dog gets to know the person who trains him extremely well. The instructor then matches the dogs up with their future owners and instructs them together for about four weeks. Every day his dogs will recognise him by sight as they see him arrive at the training centre. Even if he sees them a week or so after they have left the training centre, they are still likely to recognise him by sight. However, after a few months this will not be so, but they will recognise him when they hear his voice. After a few more months have elapsed, they will neither recognise him by sight nor by the sound of his voice, but they will recognise him by his scent. Their sense of smell never seems to fail their memories, even if several years pass by. In most cases, at the time of this recognition, the dog will act on a sudden impulse and show great excitement. This only lasts for about two minutes. The dog will then return to her master and ignore the one who originally trained her.

Living, training, and working with dogs can be one of the most fascinating things in life, and one of the greatest things about it is the wonderful companionship our dogs give us. No matter how much training we put into a dog we must always remember that he is not infallible. He is far from being like a machine—he is an animal. He is an animal whom we cannot do without.

Lastly I would like to close by reminding you all that there is something which money cannot buy, and that is the wag of a dog's tail.

Appendix

1. Australian National Kennel Council,
   Royal Show Grounds,
   Epsom Road,
   Ascot Vale,
   Victoria 3032

2. The Kennel Club,
   1 Clarges Street,
   Piccadilly,
   London W.1. Y8AB

3. The New Zealand Kennel Club (Inc)
   (Affiliated to The Kennel Club, England)
   31 Pirie Street,
   Wellington,
   New Zealand

4. The American Kennel Club,
   51 Madison Avenue,
   New York, N.Y. 10010

5. The Kennel Union of Southern Africa,
   6th Floor, Bree Castle,
   68 Bree Street,
   Cape Town 8001

Index